# My War Diary
## 1914-1918
### Ethel M. Bilbrough

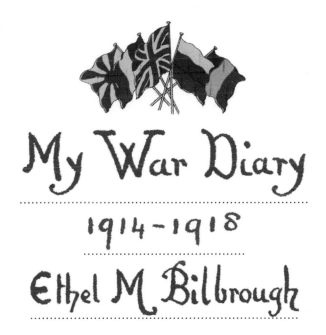

# My War Diary

## 1914–1918

### Ethel M. Bilbrough

EBURY
PRESS

1 3 5 7 9 10 8 6 4 2

Published in 2014 by Ebury Press, an imprint of Ebury Publishing

A Random House Group Company

The Random House Group Limited Reg. No. 954009

Addresses for companies within the Random House Group can be found at www.randomhouse.co.uk

A CIP catalogue record for this book is available from the British Library

To buy books by your favourite authors and register for offers visit www.randomhouse.co.uk

Design: Peter Ward

Printed and bound in China by Toppan Leefung

ISBN 9780091951115

*Half title page:* Ethel Bilbrough and her husband Kenneth.
*Frontispiece:* Ethel at Elmstead Grange, Chislehurst, with her family dog Nat, summer 1907.
Photographs on pages II, VI and VIII are provided courtesy of James J. McGrane and A. Bilbrough & Company.

# Contents

# Introduction

Imperial War Museums' vast collection provides an extraordinary connection to the First World War — from weapons and uniforms, to posters, paintings and photographs. It houses an incredible archive of letters and diaries written during this time. Their immediacy is compelling. The diary of Ethel Mary Bilbrough is amongst them. In it, she records her thoughts about what it was like to live through this devastating, transformative war.

The war extended far beyond the battlefield. Every major combatant nation had a 'home front'. In Britain, men, women and children worked in factories, donated money, and volunteered for war-related charitable organisations. Such endeavour was only possible because most people believed the nation was right to fight. This forceful moral purpose is at the heart of Ethel Bilbrough's diary, faithfully reproduced here in full.

Ethel Bilbrough was wife to Kenneth, an insurance executive whose commercial success was built on a fleet of clipper ships and marine insurance. The couple, who had no children, lived in the grand Elmstead Grange, surrounded by 22 acres of land, in Chislehurst, Kent. In a class-divided society, the wealthy, well-connected Bilbroughs were at the elite end of the spectrum. At the outbreak of the First World War, Ethel, now in her mid-forties, was a keen writer to national newspapers as well as a diarist. Her diary is interspersed with cuttings from pieces published from 'E.M.B.' offering advice about how the conflict should be conducted and endured.

The diary begins with a retrospective summary of the war's beginning, before 'real time' entries begin in 1915 through to the war's end in 1918. Ethel roves between her own experiences and a wider perspective. There are few important issues of the time that she does not comment on, from rationing and recruitment to

*Opposite left:* Ethel reading to her sister, Mary, at Elmstead Grange, 1909

*Opposite right:* Elmstead Grange, Chislehurst. Ethel witnessed the explosions at Woolwich from the turret on the right.

*Opposite below:* Elmstead Grange, Chislehurst, now Babington House School

Ethel and Kenneth on a touring holiday, early 1920s. Ethel's painting easel is stored on the rear of the car.

air raids and animals injured in military service. Her strident views are brilliantly lucid, her patriotism ardent. But, perhaps surprisingly, this shows itself through sweeping criticisms. The government, conscientious objectors who refused military service, and Britain's Allies are all subject to her wrath if they seemed to threaten victory. Her even more forceful views on Germany come as no surprise. The Kaiser is branded the 'slayer of millions'.

Ethel died in 1951. Her diary was found in a clear-out by Kenneth's second wife, Elsie, who, when offering it to the Imperial War Museum in 1961, regarded the colourful charity pins stuck within its pages as the main interest. Now, Ethel's opinions are the real draw. They crackle with vivacity. In her own view, 'It seems to me that everyone who happens to be alive in such stirring epoch-making times, ought to write *something* of what is going on!' But she is clear that the diary 'will merely be my own personal impressions'. These impressions are immensely readable, sometimes provocative, and never dull. No amount of wealth or privilege kept the First World War at bay. This spirited diary shows how the war pervaded the minds and attitudes of everyone.

Laura Clouting
Curator
Imperial War Museums

PART ONE

# Ethel M. Bilbrough, My War Diary 1914-1918

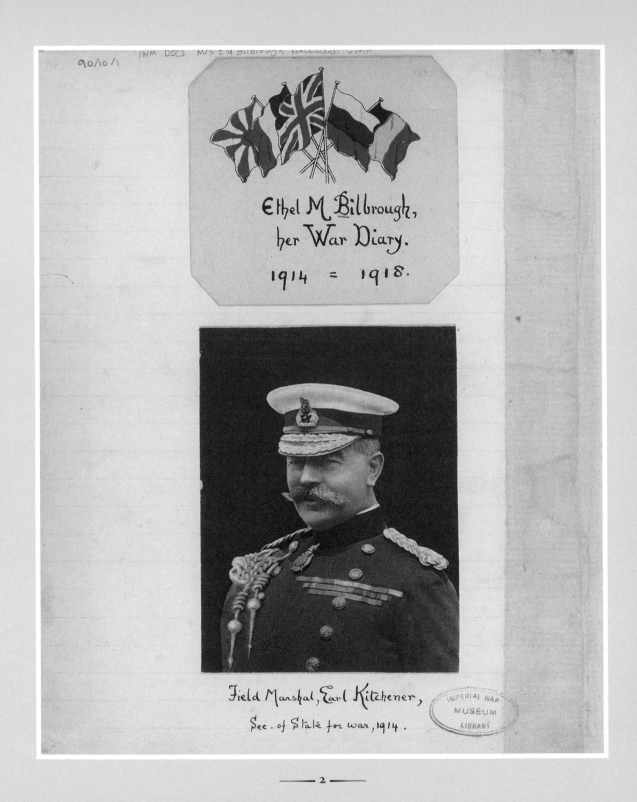

Ethel M. Bilbrough,
her War Diary.

1914 = 1918.

Field Marshal, Earl Kitchener,

Sec. of State for war, 1914.

Ethel M. Bilbrough
Elmstead Grange
Chislehurst
Kent.

July 15th, 1915.

This is going to be my war diary. I don't mean that
its to be political, or literary, or anything of that
kind, but it will merely be my own personal im-
=pressions, and I shan't even touch on the fringe
of the vast problem as to what has caused the
greatest war that has ever been known in history, or
as to what, will be likely to terminate it all!

It seems to me that every one who happens to be
alive in such stirring epoch-making times, ought to
write something of what is going on! Just think how
interesting it would be to read years hence! when peace
once more reigns supreme, and everything has settled
down to its usual torpid routine of dullness(!)

Terrible as it all is, I think I'd rather be living now
than, say in Early Victorian days! Now every one
is living and no mistake about it; there's no more
playing at things. "Life is real & life is earnest,"
and I doubt if it will ever seem quite the same
again as it did before this great European war.

One wonders now what one did in days of peace!
What did people do? What did they talk about? What

did they read about? what did they think about? (if they ever thought at all!). But moral reflections are always rather boring! and I am wondering how I will start on the difficult subject before me!

I can hardly realise that it is nearly a year ago since we were all thrown into the wildest excitement at even the prospect of a "war with Germany"! Up to the very last I don't think anyone really believed we should fight!, and I remember how staggered we were one Sunday morning last August, when walking over the common to Church, we passed a man engrossed in a Sunday paper which announced in large letters that war was proclaimed between England & Germany! Then somehow or other, it all seemed much nearer & much more real! Of course one had been following with deep interest the fighting with Servia and brave little Belgium, but that we should be drawn in, was quite another matter!

But one little realised then what it was all to mean in the future to us, the appalling loss of life, — the sacrifice, — the horror of it all! Yet it is now raging — no abatement of the cruel slaughter, it just goes on from day to day increasing in venom and hatred, and loss of life. Oh! that such a thing as war should be possible in these En-=lightened civilised (?) days!

It has evolved so gradually! Last August the state of things (as they exist now) would have been thought unspeakable! But step by step it has grown to what it now is, though in early days before the real fighting had begun, one never dreamed of such possibilities.

We went to the wilds of North Wales in September last, and expected to get right out of the war zone and all its news, and I shall never forget what an uncomfortable start it gave me when, turning a sharp corner on the isolated slopes of Snowdon one day, we were suddenly faced by a soldier in khaki with fixed bayonet, who calmly challenged us!! One felt indignant at first, then amused, & finally we replied with surprising humility (!) that we were "merely taking a walk"!!

# MEN AND WOMEN OF ENGLAND.

---

A ruthless and relentless foe seeks to grind under its heel your Country and your Liberty.

You are called upon to light your lamps of sacrifice.

To send every fit man to the Front—your Sons, your Brothers, your Friends, and to pray to God that they may return unharmed.

Your succour is wanted for those who are left behind—in money. in help, in sympathy.

---

We people of England will rise to the height of our strength and of our patriotism.

We will shew by the sacrifice we are prepared to make the value we place on the freedom of our Country and the sacredness of our homes.

By the help of God we will hand down these blessings unimpaired to our children.

We are out to Fight and to Conquer.

## For God—For King—For Country.

SEPTEMBER, 1914.

I wish I had started this book when the War actually first began! But it never entered my head then! One imagined the whole thing would be all over and forgotten in a few months. It is a great mercy that the things which are to come are veiled from us.

So I must try and go back in memory to the first early months of fighting last autumn, when it was all fresh and thrilling, with an undercurrent of Excitement and romance. One of the first things that struck me was the dreadful cruelty to the poor dear innocent horses! Men fight voluntarily, but the horses are dragged into the sickening mêlée to suffer and go through untold agonies all through no fault of their own, it seems so unfair to them.

Of course it is a most fearfully difficult question, as modern warfare is so totally different to what it was. Now the range of a battle field will extend for miles and miles, and who can be found to traverse it in order to give relief to the dying horse when there are men lying all along the line wounded and suffering? Yet if only something could be done to end the sufferings of our poor war horses who are terribly hurt, by a quick merciful death! The

**TOUCHING MEMORIAL**

By the pulpit is a small bronze model of a good, fat Army horse. And underneath is written:—

"In grateful and reverent memory of the Empire's horses (some 375,000) who fell in the Great War. Most obediently and often most painfully they died—'*Faithful unto Death, not one of them is Forgotten before God.*'"

Beautiful!

*Ten years afterwards!* . [1928]

**AN APPEAL.**

I'm only a cavalry charger,
    And I'm dying as fast as I can
(For my body is riddled with bullets—
    They've potted both me and my man);
And though I've no words to express it,
    I'm trying this message to tell
To kind folks who work for the Red Cross—
    Oh, please help the Blue one as well!

My master was one in a thousand,
    And I loved him with all my poor heart
(For horses are built just like humans,
    Be kind to them—they'll do their part),
So please send out help for our wounded,
    And give us a word in your prayers;
This isn't so strange as you'd fancy—
    The Russians do it in theirs.

I'm only a cavalry charger,
    And my eyes are becoming quite dim
(I really don't mind though I'm "done for,"
    So long as I'm going to *him*);
But first I would plead for my comrades,
    Who're dying and suffering, too—
Oh, please help the poor wounded horses!
    I'm sure that you would—if you knew.
                              SCOTS GREYS.

dreadful hideous cruelty lies in letting them die by inches ....it is too horrible to contemplate. I wrote the following letter to the Mirror and it was printed.

Of course such letters may not do one particle of good, but at least they can do no harm, and someone may read them who can help try and solve the difficulty.

And so when I feel very strongly about a thing, it is always a relief to put pen to paper!

There were answers to this, and several Societies have lately done what they can, especially the Blue Cross Society, and the Vetrinary Corps &c. But my Consolation is, that my letter came at the very commencement of the war, for I wrote it on August 11th, 1914.

**FOR THE HORSES.**

I CHANCED to be at Waterloo Station when several fine horses were patiently waiting to be taken off to the war, and the thought struck me how infinitely sad it is to contemplate the terrible pain that these poor creatures may be called upon to bear when left to die slowly, and in torment, on the battlefield.

Can no one suggest a means whereby these suffering animals could be mercifully put out of their misery at the end of an encounter?

Of course, the men come first, for whom our hearts are aching with sympathy, but have we none to spare for the friend of man, the noble cavalry horse, who has to suffer untold agony caused by shrapnel and other hideous inventions of the civilised world?

What practical effort can be made besides the expression of our sympathy in words? Perhaps some readers of *The Daily Mirror* will think out a remedy that might help in this good cause.
Chislehurst. E. M. B.

How little we dreamed last July (in 1914) of all that was impending! We had actually decided to go to Rothenburg for our Autumn holiday! and indeed it was a Very near thing, for if the war had come a few weeks later, or we had started a few weeks earlier, we should most certainly have all been taken prisoners!! How little I thought of the deadly enmity and hatred that would come so soon between ourselves and Germany as I racked my brains for a couple of hours every morning over the horrible german language in order to be able hold forth, and give orders on the Rothenburg trip! It is a mercy the future is always a sealed book. Still, things looked ominous Even from the first, and the following Entry occurs in my day diary on July 28th 1914. "Getting all the information we can "about Rothenburg, but I doubt if we shall be able to go "there after all, as owing to this fighting between Austria "and Servia there is just the hideous possibility of "an European War"!... How soon it became a hideous fact! Then poor brave little Belgium Was drawn in, and Germany began to show her poisonous fangs, and the poor Belgians Were driven right and left, homeless and destitute, and their homes pillaged and burnt. But I do love this picture! for the small Belgian is scoring off the hateful German officer — who, for once, for the moment, is helpless!

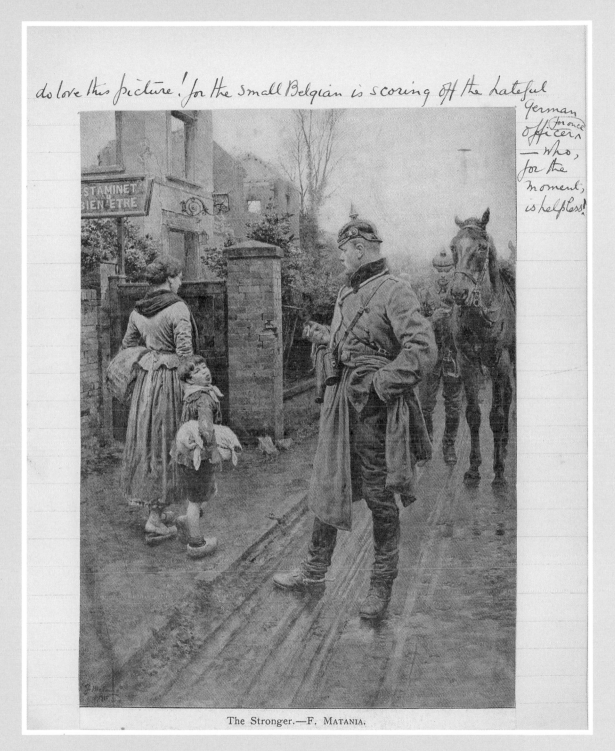

The Stronger.—F. Matania.

## II.

No sooner was England's Ultimatum to Germany given out, than stirring events came tumbling over each other's heels with amazing rapidity. France was drawn in soon after Russia, and so the dreaded European war commenced in grim earnest. Germany & Austria against the Allies of England, France, Servia, Russia, Belgium, — and later on, Italy. They had chosen a hard nut to crack, those Germans! but they have been preparing for war (especially against England) for years and years, only we never would realise or believe it!

We are always <u>late</u> in waking up to facts, and we have still much to learn as a nation.

Poor Belgium soon came to grief, though her men fought valiantly and made a noble stand against the Enemy, but they were not strong enough, and one after another — Namur, Luxemburg, Liège, and Brussels all had to be evacuated, and taken possession of by the Germans, who ceased to behave as men, and became devils. This is what war does to civilisation.

England rapidly began to change too under war conditions, yet so naturally does one thing merge into another, that one hardly comprehends all that is actually going on around us. Although such stupendous things are taking place, there are still thousands of people to whom the War has made but little material difference in their mode of life, — although of course to others it has brought suffering & sorrow & loss.

### A Year of War. July 1915.

This time last year we were on the brink of War. And such a War! It has cost the nation already many thousands of brave lives, the suffering of scores of thousands of wounded men, the desolation of many homes, and five hundred millions of pounds! But, who if told a year ago that the nation in the succeeding twelve months would suffer such things, would have expected us personally at home to have our wealth, health, and comfort interfered with so little?

So writes Mr Serle our vicar, in his Parish Magazine for July 19.15.

One cannot be thankful enough that one has no relatives fighting at the front. How awful that would be! How one would cry out against the injustice of fighting, I would cry out against even patriotism itself. Patriotism is a very fine thing in the abstract, but is it — can it ever be stronger than love? if so, then love is not "the greatest thing in the world"..... (& it is.)

EMB!

The Huns continue their cowardly dastardly attacks on poor brave little Belgium. They have not the slightest regard for the lives of women and children and even the churches are treated in the same way. They care for neither god nor the devil, — though indeed it often looks as if Germany (and especially the Kaiser!) were in league with the latter! " Here is a specimen of the havoc they delight in making of a church — this shows the altar.

A priest standing among the ruins of his once beautiful church in Termonde after its destruction by the Germans.

## GERMAN BOMBARDMENT.

On the 17ᵗʰ Dec. 1914, the Germans sent over a fleet of cruisers and bombarded our east coast towns of Scarborough, Whitby, and Hartlepool, killing many civilians, and several women, children and babies — which is apparently their idea of valour and chivalry! Over 100 lives were lost — or rather were massacred.

I suppose the last time England's shores were attacked by an enemy must have been when the Danes indulged in their "raids". But it is horrible to think that such things can take place in these enlightened (?) days, but

A house in the Crescent, Scarborough, which was shattered by a German shell fired from a Dreadnought cruiser.

then the Germans are proving every day that they
have no sense of right or justice, or morality or honour.

House in
Scarborough
where three
dead bodies
were found
after the
bombardment

## III

There is K'haki everywhere now, one is getting quite used to it. England at war! it sounds like some half forgotten fairy story of school room days, — when one sat through the long morning hours toiling drearily through the "Wars of the Roses" in "Little Arthur's History of England". // Khaki Bibles

Lord Roberts
message
to the troops.

### BIBLES FOR THE TROOPS.

### MESSAGE IN EACH FROM LORD ROBERTS.

Lord Roberts, through the medium of the Scripture Gifts Mission and the Naval and Military Bible Society, has addressed the following words to the troops on home and foreign service:—

I ask you to put your trust in God. He will watch over you and strengthen you. You will find in this little book guidance when you are in health, comfort when you are in sickness, and strength when you are in adversity.

ROBERTS, F.M.

LORD ROBERTS

& Khaki prayer books even are now bound up and sold for our soldiers, and Lord Roberts — dear good man that he was — wrote the words that I have put in above, and now they are bound up in every little khaki prayer book, — on the first page.    If only England had listened to Lord Roberts words of warning to us after the Boer War, we should be better equipped for the present desperate encounter.

# THE KAISER AND GOD.

## By BARRY PAIN.

"I rejoice with you in Wilhelm's first victory.
How magnificently God supported him!"

Led by Wilhelm, as you tell,
God has done extremely well;
You with patronizing nod
Show that you approve of God.
Kaiser, face a question new—
This—does God approve of you?

Broken pledges, treaties torn
Your first page of war adorn;
We on fouler things must look
Who read further in that book,
Where you did in time of war
All that you in peace forswore,
Where you, barbarously wise,
Bade your soldiers terrorize,
Where you made—the deed was fine—
Women screen your firing line,
Villages burned down to dust,
Torture, murder, bestial lust,
Filth too foul for printer's ink,
Crimes from which the apes would shrink—
Strange the offerings that you press
On the God of Righteousness!

Kaiser, when you'd decorate
Sons or friends who serve your State,
Not that Iron Cross bestow
But a Cross of Wood, and so—
So remind the world that you
Have made Calvary anew.

Kaiser, when you'd kneel in prayer
Look upon your hands, and there
Let that deep and awful stain
From the blood of children slain
Burn your very soul with shame,
Till you dare not breathe that Name
That now you glibly advertise—
God as one of your allies.

Impious braggart, you forget;
God is not your conscript yet;
You shall learn in dumb amaze
That His ways are not your ways,
That the mire through which you trod
Is not the high white road of God,

*To Whom, whichever way the combat rolls,*
*We, fighting to the end, commend our souls.*

## Christmas 1914

There was no talk of "a merry Christmas" this year. No one wanted to be merry even. With all the 'horrors of war, no one could feel "Christmassy".

It sounded so strange the first time we had "God save the King" sung in church as a prayer — the congregation all kneeling with bowed heads and singing it seriously, slowly, and reverently. It usually comes as a finish to mirthful festivities, or as a wind-up to some rollicking entertainment, but now that is all changed, and so has the significance of the fine old national anthem.

The next step that seem'd queer and unusual, — (and rather awesome at first) were the things we began to offer up prayers for in church every Sunday. For war hospitals; the "sick and wounded;" for "nurses"; "doctors"; "army chaplains"; for those who serve their country on sea and land", or in the air"! Then later on, lists of names were read out for those to be prayed for, and the list of sick and wounded and for dying and dead, grew so terribly long that at last it had to be divided up at the different services. As I have said, there were no Christmas festivities, and only a few people sent Christmas cards. I did an original one (symbolical), of four ships coming into port, representing the allies, with their flags "en evidence"! here it is,—

(but somehow I said the Hotchkin looked like a cracked flag, & so I cracked them out!!)

May the New Year's rising sun

Be a Herald of Peace. (but it wasn't!)

1914-15.

E.M.B

Christmas Greetings

from .............

The New Year 1915 started gloomily enough. The war
came very near indeed when three hospitals for the
wounded were opened in our own peaceful suburb
of Chislehurst. In a very short time they were full,
and at first we had all Belgians. Here french
came in useful, and I felt very thankful I could
talk it, for none of the men could speak one word of
English of course. I drove some of them out, and it
was quite entertaining, they were such nice refined
men, not a bit vulgar or common.          On the
1st of January I got up a concert for them at Holbrook,
and we had mostly french songs, though several of
the men had picked up the tune and words of
"Tipperary", and sang in the chorus lustily with their
funny broken English.               Then came the
Belgian Refugees, and again Chislehurst opened
her ever hospitable arms, and recieved several of
these poor outcasts at two beautiful houses on the
Common, prepared and furnished entirely for them,
even down to piano's! Many people took three or
four refugees into their own homes for months at a
time, a most Christian thing to do! because it is
a terrible thing to part with the peace & privacy of

one's own four walls, (whatever is happening outside them!) Chislehurst has certainly nothing to reproach itself with, for how these Belgians and the Belgian patients in the hospitals, were cared for and looked after! And concerts were got up for them constantly, and teas, and entertainments, and they were driven out in motors & carriages, and fêted, and amused, and spoilt (?) to such an extent, it's a wonder they were not all quite ruined! It proved later on not to be particularly good for them! and the teas were stopped, and the concerts more limited, and none of the men allowed to go out unless attended by someone in authority. Of course the men hated this, and they felt it fearfully undignified having to go for walks with a lady to see they didn't "get into mischief"! but then they brought it on themselves and deserved it, since when they had their liberty — they came home to the hospital on more than one occasion, extremely tipsy! so the only thing to be done was not to allow them to go out at all without an escort. Chislehurst is an exceedingly 'proper' and correct suburb, — though I suppose all small towns are alike in this respect! and there were those who disapproved of the men being

being taken out by the opposite sex, which seem'd very narrow and bigotted; and feeling rather strongly I wrote this letter to the "Mirror" which appears on this page.

Certainly I preferred the Belgians to the English Tommies, because they are innately re--fined and respectful. They never forgot at the end of a walk or a drive to salute, and say gratefully "Merci bien Madame", but the English fellows would just slope off after a walk with never a "thank you", or even a "good

E. M. Bilbrough.

morning"! But of course no one takes the poor wounded lads out for "thanks", and one has to remember that, probably, a heart of real English gold beats under the undemonstrative English Khaki coat!

On the 7th May (1915) all Europe was thrown into a state of consternation at a diabolical act of the German fiends! They actually torpedoed (and sank,) one of our largest liners, the "Lusitania" coming from America; and twelve hundred civilians – American, English, and many other harmless and helpless people were ruthlessly drowned without a chance of escape.

Words entirely fail to express what all England – – and America too – felt at this unparalled outrage. America talked a lot, and threatened Germany if such a thing "Ever occurred again", but it all ended in smoke, and was soon forgotten – except by the poor sorrowing relatives of the 12,00 souls whose bodies lay at the bottom of the sea, all because Germany is at war. The relentless wickedness of such an act has not its like in all history I should think.

But the Germans become more inhuman every day.

One of the strangest things in life is, how soon one becomes used to a new and altered state of Circumstances! For instance, on going up to London now, say on a Saturday to dine and go to a theatre, Everything is quite different to what it was before the war. There are fewer trains, and the ones which do continue to run are horribly crowded. The passengers are mostly men in Khaki. Young Subalterns, and officers, and colonels, all passing on their way to the front, with no idea as to whether they will ever return to the old country again, or rest (for all time) in foreign lands.

At the restaurants too, Every table has its boy or full-fledged man in the Khaki uniform which has become so common. Some of the tables are occupied by wounded soldiers, and the last time we were at the "Coventry" having dinner, there was next to us, a young fellow calmly enjoying himself with the whole of his head bound up in a white bandage! yet no one Even glanced at him, though a year ago he would probably have been politely asked by the manager to vacate his seat!! Then returning after dark, Everything is changed. London is thrown into complete obscurity on account of a possible Zepplin raid! Instead of the brilliantly lit up streets, the rows of coloured lights at the various music halls and cinemas, the electric lights everywhere, their reflection flickering in the river along the Embankment, now all is plunged in comparative darkness. Only a light where it is absolutely necessary, and it is positively dangerous to cross the roads. Directly dusk appears, all the blinds have to be pulled down in the trains for fear of hostile aircraft, & one reads this in every railway carriage

## SOUTH EASTERN AND CHATHAM RAILWAY.

# IMPORTANT NOTICE.

Passengers are requested to see that the Blinds in this Compartment are pulled down after dark, except while the Train is standing at the Station.

This is necessary in order to conform to the requirements of the Government.

Much continues to be talked and written about on the subject of Economy in war time. It is very necessary, for the price of Every thing continues to go up so alarmingly, and taxation is becoming heavier and heavier, in order to meet the appalling demands the War makes upon us. The government is now spending three million a day; it is difficult to take in all that such a sum means.    But Extravagance is at all times a silly and ostentatious thing. We should be much happier if we all lived simpler lives whether with a view to saving for the country or otherwise, and its really rather a good thing that people are now forced "to pull up" whether they like it or not! England had been getting fearfully luxurious and selfindulgent and, it is to be feared, rather slack and Effeminate too, and nothing short of an awful War like this would have brought her as a nation to her senses. (& her knees)

When the war ends, I wonder if people will keep on with their new cautious way of living? or whether they will return recklessly to former Extravagances and with renewed zeal for having been obliged to discontinue it for so long a time! But certainly people are happier when they cease to be Epicures and

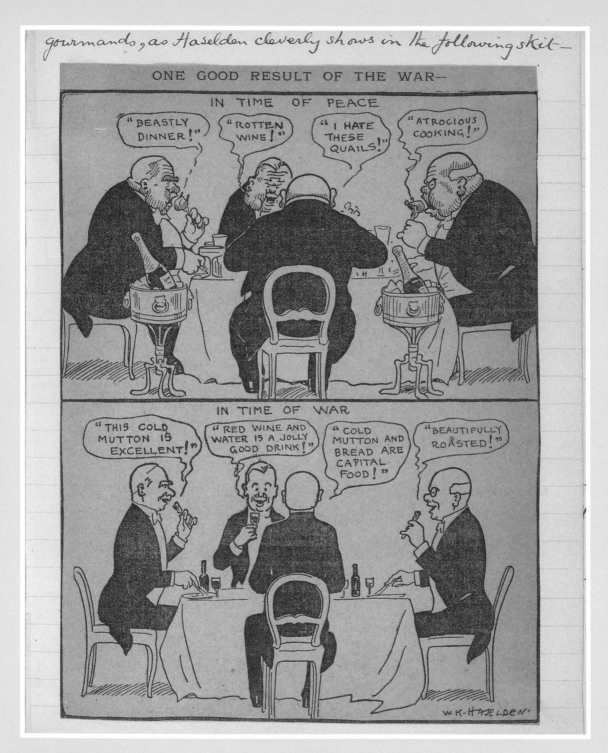

**Money Must be Saved.**

To give additional assistance to the Government it was necessary, said Mr. A. Bilbrough at the meeting of the London and South-Western Bank, that the most rigid economy must be practised, and much of the money which they were accustomed to spend without thought and as a matter of course must be saved. "Never have such wages," said the chairman, with emphasis, "been paid to our workmen as are now ruling. I wish that I could add: 'And never has so large a proportion been laid aside for a rainy day.'" (Hear, hear.)

Times were bad after every war, added Mr. Bilbrough, and unless large accumulations of capital were made the times would press more heavily than before.

A. Bilbrough Esq^re on saving.

It will be a thousand pities if we drift back into the old spendthrift ways directly peace is proclaimed, though in truth that day seems a long way off, for we are still in a very dark tunnel, where, however much we may strain our eyes, no sign of the end can be seen.

People love to speculate on how long this war will last! Some say '6 months', others "another year", but I believe it will be a good while longer. Germany will hold on like a bull dog to her last gasp, and the English and French will never give in, — at least one hopes not! — so there we are! and there we shall remain apparently, as long as there are any men left alive to fight!

Its a pity women don't fight, — (I mean more than they do!!)

E.M.Bilbrough to The Mirror.

**SOCIAL SIMPLICITY.**

ONE result of the war is that we find less extravagance, less luxury than formerly, but there is still room for improvement in this direction.

For instance, our evenings at home might be made much more attractive than they are at very small cost.

Why is it that we so seldom care to ask our friends in to partake of a little informal homely dinner, to be followed by music or games?

Simply because we know what these "little dinners" mean—a five or six course meal with wines handed round, all of which entails expense and extra work and worry for both hostess and servants. Yet no one in what may be termed middle-class society dares to break through this tiresome and foolish convention; but the war may give us a chance to do so.

How sensible and pleasant it would be if we and our neighbours came to a definite understanding when asking one another round to dine quietly at each other's houses that only a very simple meal would be provided—say, soup or fish, meat and sweets. There would be no need for any fuss or upsetting of the domestic machinery, we should see far more of our friends than we do at present, and with them spend many a sociable evening.

A hearty welcome, a plain, well-cooked dinner and pleasant companionship is all that is really necessary to promote a thoroughly enjoyable evening. E. M. B.
(Bilbrough.

Wednesday 30ᵗʰ June. 1915

Today was the day set apart to collect funds for our allies, the French. Flags were sold in every street and huge sums of money were collected. Where all the money comes from is a marvel! the calls upon it are colossal yet it never seems to run dry, and the Prince of Wale's Fund — for those who suffer" by reason of the war", has now reached a total of over five million pounds. Certainly this War — awful as it is, is bringing out all the generosity and christian charity there is in the world, with a Vengeance!

There is a great deal talked about the "Entent Cordiale" just now between us and the French, — I wonder if its cordiality of an abiding nature?! These little medals were also sold to day for the French Red Cross Fund, and most of the men wore one in their coats.

French relief fund medals.

By hindering the output of munitions of war the workmen on strike are playing the part of the Kaiser's friend.

## August. 1915.

A warm weary month, when people's hearts were sinking at the prospect of another winter's war. For surely this terrible fighting will continue; there is no sign of a rift in the clouds, and the pessimist looks glum, and the optimist is silent. War — war — war, and our brave lads are being hacked and shot-down day by day in appalling numbers. One wonders if there will be any men left at all in the world at the present rate of extermination? it will be a world of women before long, — what an awful place !!

There was much talk this month as to whether it was justifiable to take a holiday or not as usual, & I think everyone agreed that it was more necessary than ever this year, when men's hearts are failing them — Things do not look bright, and no one can foresee the end of it all. They say that the Kaiser, — that slayer of millions, — has aged 20 years since this war began, and he now looks worn and haggard and weary; — and well he may !

Our losses are heavy. They were bound to be. We shall bear them stoically, as is our duty, not inquiring whether any could have been avoided until the time comes for such inquiry, but remembering that, heavy as is the toll of life, it is less than that of our Allies, and far less than that of the enemy. Therein lies our hope for the future. We have lost in killed in round numbers seventy thousand men; the most trustworthy estimates of the German losses indicate that their total of killed reaches well over a million, and their rate of loss, which has been heavier than that of all the Allies throughout, continues disproportionately heavy.

1915

Thursday 7th October. 1915.

Two months since I wrote in this book! and yet everything
is going on in the same dreary drawnout manner, and the
death roll of our "brave manly English boys" increasing
horribly day by day. We have been away for our autumn
holiday, but the war dogged our footsteps, and once while
placidly sketching on the cliff, a khaki sentinel approached
me and calmly demanded my sketch book, as sketching was
forbidden within three miles of the coast! I had to give it up of course,
but relieved myself by saying some most unchristian things!

MEMORANDUM.                    Army Form C. 348.

From  O.C. Byclist Detachment
      Portland Garrison.
        The Nothe,
          Weymouth
To   Miss E. M. Bilbrough
      Chiselhurst
        Kent

    29th July 1915.

  Herewith please find
the sketch book taken
from you at Lulworth
Cove.

But after a few weeks I got
my sketch book back safe &
sound, with the accompanying
notice! and it amused one to
think what a lot of trouble
these good people had given
themselves over a practically,
empty, and harmless little
sixpenny sketchbook! How-
ever, it has given me another momento of the war to stick in here!

# NATIONS AT WAR.

## NEARLY THE WHOLE OF EUROPE ENGAGED.

With the declaration of war by Italy on Bulgaria, the only nations in Europe not now engaged in the present gigantic struggle are Spain, Rumania, Holland, Switzerland, Greece, Denmark, Sweden, and Norway.

It was on July 28 last year that Austria threw down the gauntlet, and opened hostilities with Serbia. Thereafter events developed in the following dramatic fashion:—

1914.
Aug. 1.—Germany declares war on Russia.
  „  3.—Germany  „  „  „ France.
  „  4.—Britain  „  „  „ Germany.
  „  10.—France  „  „  „ Austria.
  „  12.—Britain  „  „  „ Austria.
  „  23.—Japan  „  „  „ Germany.
Nov. 5.—Britain  „  „  „ Turkey.
1915.
May 23.—Italy  „  „  „ Austria.
Aug. 20.—Italy  „  „  „ Turkey.
Oct. 15.—Britain  „  „  „ Bulgaria.
  „  16.—France  „  „  „ Bulgaria.
  „  19.—Italy  „  „  „ Bulgaria.

Serbia was attacked by Bulgaria without any declaration of war. The other members of the Entente—Belgium and Montenegro—are also at war with our enemies, while the little Republic of San Marino declared herself on Italy's side. Portugal has also declared war on Germany.

# Italian Flag Day.

## Thursday 7th Oct. (con)

Today was the Italian Flag Day, and London was full of the little penny flags of Italy's colours. One little flag (just like the one I give here) below) was sold for fifty pounds! but of course all the money went to help Italy and her soldiers as they are now our allies, though comparatively recent ones. I think the English nation is a most remarkably generous one. Only the other day they were "shelling" out for the French red cross day, and now the English man's hand is once more in his pocket for Italy! It is wonderful, simply wonderful where all the money comes from! People have only to ask and they get fortunately

Now that Italy has thrown in her part with our Allies, and that Bulgaria has thrown in her lot against us with Turkey, nearly all Europe is now fighting in this ghastly war, as will be easily seen by the printed list on opposite page to this.

### Wednesday 13th Oct. 1915

Being the night of our harvest festival, A. and I went
to church, as, war or no war, theres no reason why people
shouldn't be grateful for a splendid harvest.

It was a lovely night — not a cloud to be seen;
a fine night for Zeppelins, and an ideal one for a
raid! So it proved; for on coming out of church
after a nice peaceful service about "ploughing fields"
and "harvest homes", we found Chislehurst in a most
unusual state of commotion! Excited groups hung about
the church porch, & we caught fragmentary bits of con-
=versation about "bombs", and "shells", and "guns"!

In spite of the myriads of stars it was very dark
there being no moon, — goodness knows where it had
got to, (scared away I should think by the attrocity
of mankind!) Coming home one found it expedient
to walk in the middle of the road, which seem'd the
only place where one couldn't break one's ankle
over on the unseen curb, or barge into a gate or
a lamp-post! — none of which are lit now owing
to the new lighting regulations. Coming along
Willow grove we met a man (in a state of
abject terror,) who stopped us and asked if we

had "seen the Zepplins"? He was an extremely poor and common man! but Excitement (& danger) makes everyone equal!

Things seem'd to quiet down after that, and as we walked down Walden Road and came out at the opening at the end, there was nothing to be seen but a great arc of indigo blue sky scintillating with countless stars. A few stragglers hung about the lodges as if half hoping to hear another gun! but it was all as silent as the grave, and we slipped quietly in to the Grange as the servants were all abed (that sounds nice & old fashioned!) and retired for the night. But somehow I couldn't sleep to save my life, everything was quiet; but I heard imaginary noises & held my breath listening. So an hour or two passed, and then quite audibly & quite unmistakably a canon went off, bang—bang, bang bang bang!! and (extremely alarmed) I woke up Ken sleeping the sleep of the just! A Zepplin raid either makes a person intensely valiant, or a pitiful coward!!

Ken was annoyed at being disturbed, and muttering something about "Gott strafen the Kaiser," turned over & went to sleep again! But the great guns at Woolwich (only six miles away) went on thundering away, and I wondered what was going on, and whether destruction and suffering & loss of life were really & truly taking place so near at hand. Things in the paper always seem so far away, its only when one sees and hears for oeself, that the real horrors of war becomes apparent. Then presently amid the booming of guns, came a terrific sort of explosion, like a crash of several canon going off altogether, and whatever it was, I knew it was something deathly, — probably a bomb, and out of bed I hopped & lit a candle. The air seem'd alive with horrid weird uncanny sounds, and there is something terrifying in the thought that two miles up above one in space there is a merciless enemy dropping incendiary bombs promiscuously on whatever comes handy!!

Ken actually did get up then (of his own free will!) & got into a dressing gown, & we went into the oriel room in the dark.—

There the window was all alight with the reflection of search lights, and shells from our guns being hurled up into the sky trying to reach the Zepplin, and then as we got to the window, a shell burst just like a firework, with a lurid red light. But we never reach the Zepplins, which (two miles high) merely look down on our breaking shells fathoms below, & laugh!

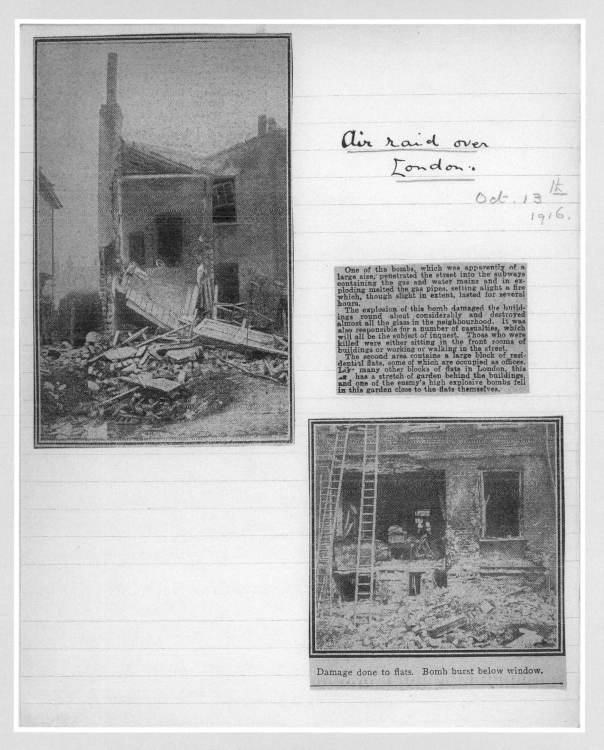

Air raid over
London.

Oct. 13th
1916.

One of the bombs, which was apparently of a large size, penetrated the street into the subways containing the gas and water mains and in exploding melted the gas pipes, setting alight a fire which, though slight in extent, lasted for several hours.

The explosion of this bomb damaged the buildings round about considerably and destroyed almost all the glass in the neighbourhood. It was also responsible for a number of casualties, which will all be the subject of inquest. Those who were killed were either sitting in the front rooms of buildings or working or walking in the street.

The second area contains a large block of residential flats, some of which are occupied as offices. Like many other blocks of flats in London, this as has a stretch of garden behind the buildings, and one of the enemy's high explosive bombs fell in this garden close to the flats themselves.

Damage done to flats. Bomb burst below window.

It was horribly cold standing there shivering in the dark room & watching weird things going on in the heavens, and Ken soon observed that he was "going back to bed". As there seem'd nothing else to be done I followed suit, but sleep didn't come for the rest of the night, and I was very thankful to see the early dawn steal through the curtains and know that this nightmare of a night was ended. But the Zepplins wrought havoc, and forty two people failed to escape, eight were killed, and the others seriously hurt. Bombs were dropped on Woolwich where much damage was done (that was the strange uncanny sound I heard) and about 40 fell on Croydon, while London was fiercely attacked. One side of the Strand was completely wrecked, and Ken said he went and saw where one bomb had fallen in the street, and there was a hole in the solid concrete, four ft. deep! — it had gone through like a red hot needle in a piece of butter! No wonder people are afraid of such demoniacal inventions, they would go slick through a house and anything (or anyone) who came in their way! All the trains were held up so that their light should be no guide, and the 8 o'clock train from town never got to Elmstead till 1 o'clock! I heard

it come in, but little thought what train it was!
X (the train) made an impression on me, for after the strain
& anxiety of listening to unknown & terrifying
sounds, — sounds never heard before, —, the puffing & snorting
of a railway train sounded friendly & sympathetic,
& gave one a feeling of security & relief!

Next day the papers made light of it all, saying
only 8 were killed and 30 wounded, but that was
only up to 11.30. I felt there would be fresh re-
=velations after 12 o'clock. Later on it was
announced there were no fewer than 170
casualties, & over 40 deaths which is awful;
— five were children. Many parts of London
were wrecked, including part of the Lyceum theatre
where some people were killed, and part of the
Strand is in a state of complete ruin. Bombs were
simply rained down on Croydon where eight
people were killed in one house, and at Woolwich
(near here) great damage was done, and bombs
went clean through two churches there. So
that was what we heard! not merely the firing of
our canon at the Zepplins, but their own
dastardly murderous bombs falling & exploding
on our innocent civileans
within a few miles of us.

—— 45 ——

## AIR RAIDS TO DATE. *to October 13th 1915.*

Following is a record of the Zeppelin raids this year:— *1915*

| | Kld. | Injd. |
|---|---|---|
| January 19.—Yarmouth and district | 4 | 9 |
| February 21.—Colchester and Braintree | — | — |
| April 14.—Tyneside | — | 2 |
| April 16.—Lowestoft and Maldon | — | — |
| April 29.—Ipswich and Bury St. Edmunds | — | — |
| May 10.—Southend district | 1 | — |
| May 17.—Ramsgate | 2 | 8 |
| May 27.—Southend | 3 | — |
| May 31.—Outlying London | 6 | — |
| June 4.—E. and S. East Coasts | — | — |
| June 6.—East Coast | 24 | 40 |
| June 15.—North-East Coast | 16 | 14 |
| August 9.—East Coast | 15 | 14 |
| August 12.—East Coast | 6 | 23 |
| August 17.—Eastern Counties | 10 | 36 |
| September 7.—Eastern Counties | 17 | 39 |
| September 8.—Eastern Counties and London district | 38 | 124 |
| September 11.—East Coast | — | — |
| September 12.—East Coast | — | — |
| September 13.—East Coast | — | — |
| October 13.—London area | 8 | 34 |

*41 . 109*

*First year of the war; and Zeppelin raids only (not the deadly subsequent Gothas)*

Of course there comes up now the grave question as to whether we should adopt their villanous methods and drop bombs on their innocent women & children. At first it is a revolting thought and entirely re-=pugnant to an Englishman's idea of warfare. Yet something must be done to put a stop to this diabolical murder, and if we retaliated it might bring these raids to an end. The German hatred to us is Colossal! and the picture below depicts it cleverly.

STUDY OF A PRUSSIAN HOUSEHOLD HAVING ITS MORNING HATE.

NURSE·EDITH·CAVELL

Tragedies follow each other in quick succession now-a-days. Just now all England is boiling with wrath at the cold blooded murder of one of our British nurses in Belgium. Edith Cavell her name was, and she has been sheltering and befriending English & French soldiers in Belgium and helping them rejoin their regiments. Of course she knew she was defying german law! a very risky thing to attempt! She was imprisoned, tried, and almost before anyone knew anything about it, she was calmly shot in the night, or rather at 2 o'clock in the morning. What a ghastly time to be executed!

She was very brave and heroic, and declared she was "happy to die for her country," but poor soul! her courage failed her, at the thought of those deadly six rifles awaiting her, and as she walked to the place of execution, she fainted. The courageous noble minded(!) man who was in charge, calmly drew his revolver and shot her dead where she lay. What a glorious triumph for Germany! to shoot a poor fainting hospital nurse! — a woman who had given all her life to the care of others.

This incident has made a perfect furore, and

a memoral fund is being started to perpetuate the memory of this noble "martyr"! Still, I think its all being rather over done, and we shouldn't like a german woman in England getting her countrymen (who were prisoners) back to the Fatherland! But we shouldn't shoot her like a dog for all that.

Three lines of conduct, and three only, are before us to-day: to fight, to assist the fighters, and to tend those who have fallen in the fight.

Nurse Edith Cavell, assassinated by the Germans in defiance of every law, divine and human. The Kaiser could have prevented the crime, but chose to permit it, and is chiefly responsible.

Map showing English War hospitals in the midland counties in Oct. 1915

IN HONOUR OF OUR WOUNDED 1915

### Thursday 21<sup>st</sup> October 1915.

Today is "our day", that is to say a day for
our Red Cross Fund, and surely one could have
no better object for any fund than that which looks
after our wounded, — who alas! are increasing at
a terrible rate, as the distribution of red cross
hospitals on the opposite page goes to prove.

One thing always strikes me as being so horrible,
and that is the fact of our poor wounded men
being sent out again directly they are well enough
to the horrors of the battle field, which they already know
to their cost, while there are several great lazy
louts of fellows who have done (and are doing)
absolutely nothing for their country. But there
is no doubt that before long, we shall have Conscription
in England.    Kitchener's appeal
has been nobly responded to, and our
men — our true men — have given
up everything to uphold our honour, —
for its come to that. But still we need men, —
and more & more men.

King George's letter to his people.

The text of the King's letter is as follows:

Buckingham Palace.

**TO MY PEOPLE.**

At this grave moment in the struggle between my people and a highly-organised enemy, who has transgressed the laws of nations and changed the ordinance that binds civilised Europe together, I appeal to you.

I rejoice in my Empire's effort, and I feel pride in the voluntary response from my subjects all over the world who have sacrificed home, fortune and life itself in order that another may not inherit the free Empire which their ancestors and mine have built.

I ask you to make good these sacrifices.

The end is not in sight. More men and yet more are wanted to keep my armies in the field, and through them to secure victory and enduring peace.

In ancient days the darkest moment has ever produced in men of our race the sternest resolve.

I ask you, men of all classes, to come forward voluntarily and take your share in the fight.

In freely responding to my appeal, you will be giving your support to our brothers who, for long months, have nobly upheld Britain's past traditions and the glory of her arms.

**GEORGE, R.I.**

There is a rumour in the air that sooner or later we must have conscription! After all other countries have it and I don't see why we should be exempt, and let a lot of lazy loafers hang about at home while others braver and better are doing their work. But I doubt if the present government would dare demand a big thing like conscription! especially as its a stupid shifting vacillating sort of government, that can't make up its mind what to do, & it has made hideous irretrievable blunders, — Such for instance as the Dardenelle affair, a disgrace & a cruel wanton waste of brave men's lives, which are so precious today we cannot value them enough.

It is not often that one is touched personally by the war in comparatively small matters. But there is one way we are affected by it which is exceedingly annoying. It is when one recieves a letter like this! ←

**OPENED BY CENSOR.**

**629**

If there is one thing more than another that a man feels a private personal right to, it is his own letters!! But the enclosed reached one the other day, which shows how our old traditions are all being uprooted. To have strange prying curious eyes reading one's own letters (that concern no one else) is exasperating!!!

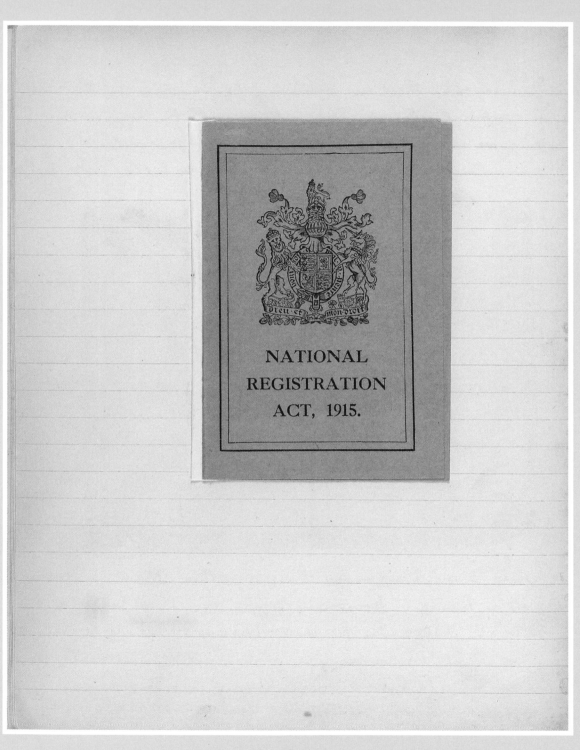

NATIONAL
REGISTRATION
ACT, 1915.

This is to Certify that

(a) Mr. Ethel Mary Gillbrough

(b) Household Duties

30.

(c) of Elmstead Grange
Chislehurst

has been Registered under the
NATIONAL REGISTRATION
ACT, 1915.

Signature of Holder. }

GOD SAVE THE KING.

(a) Name.  (b) Occupation.  (c) Postal Address.

BOROUGH OF BROMLEY. KENT.

For some reason best known to those in authority, there has been an immense universal Registration Act passed throughout the country & every man and woman has had to give their names ages & occupations — (old men & old women being exempt ) Anyhow as its got something to do with the war I shall stick my card in here as its my war diary, besides I've no use for the silly thing, & why do they put "household duties" as my principal occupation in life when they certainly constitute the least? Just as if one was a german (yh) frau, (yh) frau, or a care wo "a martha"!!!

No two figures attracted greater attention yesterday than King George and the German Emperor, who came to England to mark his love for his kinsman and that kinsman's realm by riding in the solemn procession, even as nine years since he rode behind the gun-carriage on which were the mortal remains of Queen Victoria. The picture shows King George (in the centre); the Duke of Connaught, the late King's brother (nearest the camera); and the Kaiser.—(*Daily Mirror* photograph.)

May 21st 1910.

The other day I was rumaging among a lot of old newspapers, and found a "Daily Mirror" of the date of King Edward VII^th — giving details and pictures of his funeral. In these days, the accompanying picture is of interest. How horrified the poor dead King would have been if he could have foreseen what horrors and devilment were to emanate from the "sorrowing kinsman"(?) behind his coffin."

I give the picture on the opposite page. Oh how little our poor grieving royal family knew then what a Judas, what a serpent was there, in the very midst of them all! He was a Judas even down to the kiss.

(see below)

May 21^st 1910

March 5th.

Conscription in England has come! One can hardly realise it, things have come about so gradually. Voluntary recruiting did well, but not well enough, and the slackers had to be got at somehow, so thanks to Lord Derby's scheme, all those who wouldn't enlist will be made to. But the government have felt their way to this great step very cautiously, very guardedly, and have made absurd concessions relating to men bearing arms who may have "conscientious" objections to war! and endless exemptions are being made. On these lax lines of course things are not working, & far more stringent rules must be enforced if we are to get the necessary men. Naturally every coward and slacker thinks fighting is "wrong"! and the most ludicrous reasons are being put forward by men who want to get exemption owing to their conscientious[!]scruples! The other day a man who said he was an artist, claimed exemption on the grounds that he "could not mutilate anything so beautiful as the human form"!!

Only the single men have been called up so far, but compulsory service is soon to be put into practise for the young married men also.

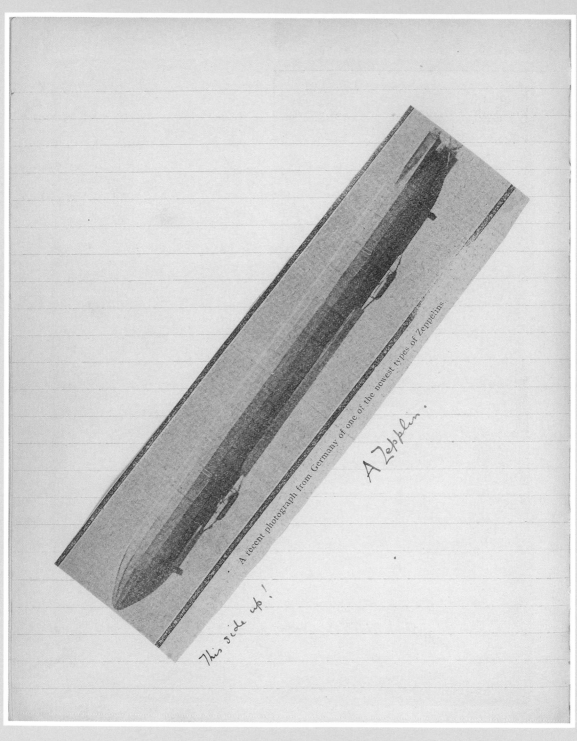

A recent photograph from Germany of one of the newest types of Zeppelins.

A Zepplin.

This side up!

A Zepplin dropping bombs.

This is really a most extraordinary photograph! It was taken during one of the actual raids on London! There are the search lights on it, and if you look closely, you can see the bombs in the act of falling from the Zepplin to the Earth.

These most vile implements of modern warfare have been rife lately, and rarely a month — or even a week passes — without a barbarous raid on some perfectly peaceful town or village, by means of which about 200 people (many of them children and babies) have been done to death, to say nothing of those who have been injured & maimed for life. What a degrading war this is, besides being a blood thirsty & terrible one. The poisonous gasses, the Zepplins, the torpedoes, and the hidden treacherous mines, all strike a note of mean unfairness; in modern slang its simply "not cricket". But what does that matter to the Huns who have lost all semblance of humanity?

**WAR TIME CROP IN A CHURCHYARD.**

Potatoes instead of flowers are being grown in the churchyard of St. Catherine's, Neasdon, the vicar, curate and members of the congregation acting as sowers and reapers.

# May. 1916

The most lovely month of the whole year!
and never has there been a more beautiful
May than this one. Yet while the birds sing,
and the Cuckoo's note is heard continually,
the sound of canon practising intermingle
with the harmony of spring. For war still
rages, and people have given up saying "when
peace comes," or "when the war is ended," for
at the present moment there does not appear the
slightest possibility of things being settled.

Our government does nothing but wrangle
and procrastinate; there has been a serious
rebellion in Ireland and several people
have been killed and wounded and shot, just
as if we hadn't enough on hand without party
politics and strife! Never were things
in such a hopeless tangle. "Compulsion for all"
has been finally decided on, after several half-
hearted attempts at it. They introduced it at
first in a pitifully weak way, allowing conscientious
objectors not to join the ranks! Of course there

immediately hundreds of consciences awoke that
had previously been dormant. But now that
is all stopped, and every man will have to
do something for England provided he is not past
the age limit — ie 45. (thank goodness K. is!)
    Lately a home has been opened by Arthur
Pearson for those blinded in this ghastly war,
and Ken has been working hard for it. He
has now raised 12,000 pounds, really a
colossal sum in these hard times. There was
a notice in all the papers and the Daily
Graphic had his picture — not half bad!
here it is —, he didn't want it to go in, but
                                    I did!

## A WONDERFUL COLLECTION.

### Generosity to Blinded Sailors and Soldiers

Mr. Kenneth Bilbrough, a member of Lloyd's,
has during the last few weeks raised no less
a sum than £11,200 for the benefit of the blinded
sailors and soldiers at St. Dunstan's.

The contributors have all been connected with
the commercial and insurance world, and include
most of the shipping companies in the kingdom
The fact that Mr. Bilbrough was a schoolfellow
of Mr. C. Arthur Pearson, at Winchester College,
led him to start his collection, which prospered
in a manner exceeding his most sanguine hopes.
The first contributor was another Old Wykehamist.

The substantial help which has been thus secured will be principally devoted to the fund
which is to be invested for the after care of the
men who have been trained at St. Dunstan's.

Mr. Kenneth Bilborough,
who has raised £11,200 recently for the blinded soldiers.
(Photographed by Swaine.)
(11,200)

One cutting out of many! (He finally collected
seventy two thousand pounds
for S. Dunstans)

Daily Graphic
6th May

## 21st May 1916.

The latest excitement has been the Daylight Saving Bill. Some years ago the originator of the scheme, one Willet by name who lived at Chislehurst, tried hard to get the government to adopt it, but with their usual dislike of venturing on anything new — (even should it be of the utmost benefit to mankind!) they would have none of it. But now that poor Willet has been in his grave some years, and as the war has brought home to our tardy stupid government the utmost need of saving coal and gas, the Bill was not only been thought advisable, but brought in and passed. So on Saturday night, or rather on Sunday morning the 21st May, at 2 o'clock, all clocks and watches had to be set on to 3 o'clock! We altered all our time pieces however at 9.30 on Sat. evening, and then went to bed as we had made it 10.30!! So we got all right without any difficulty, and without any loss of sleep! Though there were several dolts in England who "raised objections". I believe there are people who will want to argue and make objections when the Last Day comes!! We benefit in many ways by the new arrangement. To begin with, in hot summer it is delightful to find at 8.30 in the morning that the air is quite bracing and fresh (it being in reality only 7.30'.) and you can open every window for an hour, & so cool the house for the whole day. Then if one is shopping at 12 o'clock — usually the hottest time of the day, one is surprised to find how fresh it is, for of course its only eleven! But the greatest benifit of all is after dinner, when it is now broad day light till close on ten! and instead of having to get the gas lit + sit reading in doors, one can just go for a good walk, or do some gardening, or indulge in any other day light occupation. Taking it all round, every one has reason to bless the name of Willet!

The "Kindly matron":

EXCELLENT IN INTENTION

NOT REALLY WANTED

"The Elderly Spinster":

BUT THIS ONE MAY WRITE AS OFTEN AS SHE LIKES

W·K· HASELDEN

June 2nd

It has been the fashion lately for members of the feminine sex to write letters to so called lonely soldiers in the trenches! The formality of any introduction is dispensed with, & a girl may write to any Tommy or young officer she likes. A cool request from some "lonely soldier" made my blood boil! & I answered it.

**THEIR LETTERS.**

I CANNOT help feeling that any inclination one may have felt to write to "Lonely Soldier" has been somewhat damped by his letter in *The Daily Mirror*. It is fairly obvious that the letter he likes "best of all" has nothing whatever to do with the art of penmanship. It is just the writer, the little "dream maiden," who is the attraction. Although her letter may be "crammed with cheery optimism," I venture to ask if "Lonely Soldier" would care twopence about it if he knew the sender happened to be some kindly matron or an elderly spinster anxious to do her bit.

After all, "pen letters" were asked for, but the kind of letter presumably was not specified. If a correspondence is desired merely as a means to an end in promoting the opening chapter to a "whole romantic novel," it would be more to the point if a kind of war-corresponding-matrimonial agency could be started, it being understood that no "boyish flappers," and no one over thirty need apply!
E. M. B.

These illustrations by Haselton, appeared the day after my letter in the Mirror!

73

## Saturday 3rd June. 1916

This morning comes news of our first naval battle in the great war, for up to now the germans have kept their fleet well boxed up in port. We have lost heavily, as our main fleet was not in the north sea where Admiral Beattie's squad=ron was attacked by the Enemy, with her most powerful battle ships, cruisers, and torpedos, aided by three Zepplins to throw search lights &c, & to guide them which way to go. A most unequal fight to start with, & our splendid "Queen Mary" sank in two minutes, and others followed suit before the main fleet could get up to their assistence. Our losses were appalling, about five thousand four hundred killed, where as in the great [!] battle of Trafalgar only about 400 lives were lost, — far less than there were on the "Queen Mary" alone, which had over 1,000 souls. And it's dreadful to think of the poor little "middys" lads of sixteen having to go through what must have been a veritable hell upon earth. Two Admirals killed, & 333 officers. All England is bewailing, and no wonder.

## June 7th 1916.

The worst news we have had since the war began, reached us today, and all England is electrified with the shock — sudden & awful — that Lord Kitchener is drowned. He and his principal staff were on their way to visit Russia, & when off the Orkneys at night, and in a rough sea & gale of wind, some evil german submarine torpedoed and sank the vessel they were on, and none were saved except two of the ships crew, who were unable to throw any light on the disaster. It has been a sad blow to England, for Kitchener was a fine man; & who but he could have raised a voluntary army of five million men? Everyone is feeling de= =pressed and down-hearted, for the War-Lord was so trusted, and in a fierce struggle like the present war which is a struggle to the death, it is a bad thing to lose a trusted leader.

Some hours after the sad news reached England, it was all contradicted, & declared to be a mistake! and that made the disappointment all the worse when it was finally proved to be true after all.

# WHAT SAVED THE DELICATE DAUGHTER.

Work! Life-giving work! Instead of moping about the house, or chattering all day, thousands of well-to-do women who fancied themselves invalids have found "something to do" since the war began, and are all the healthier and happier for it.—(By Mr. W. K. Haselden.)

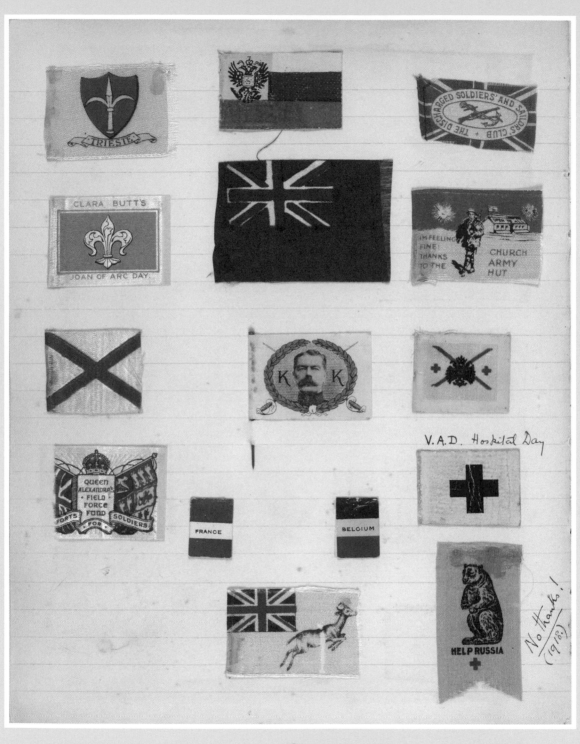

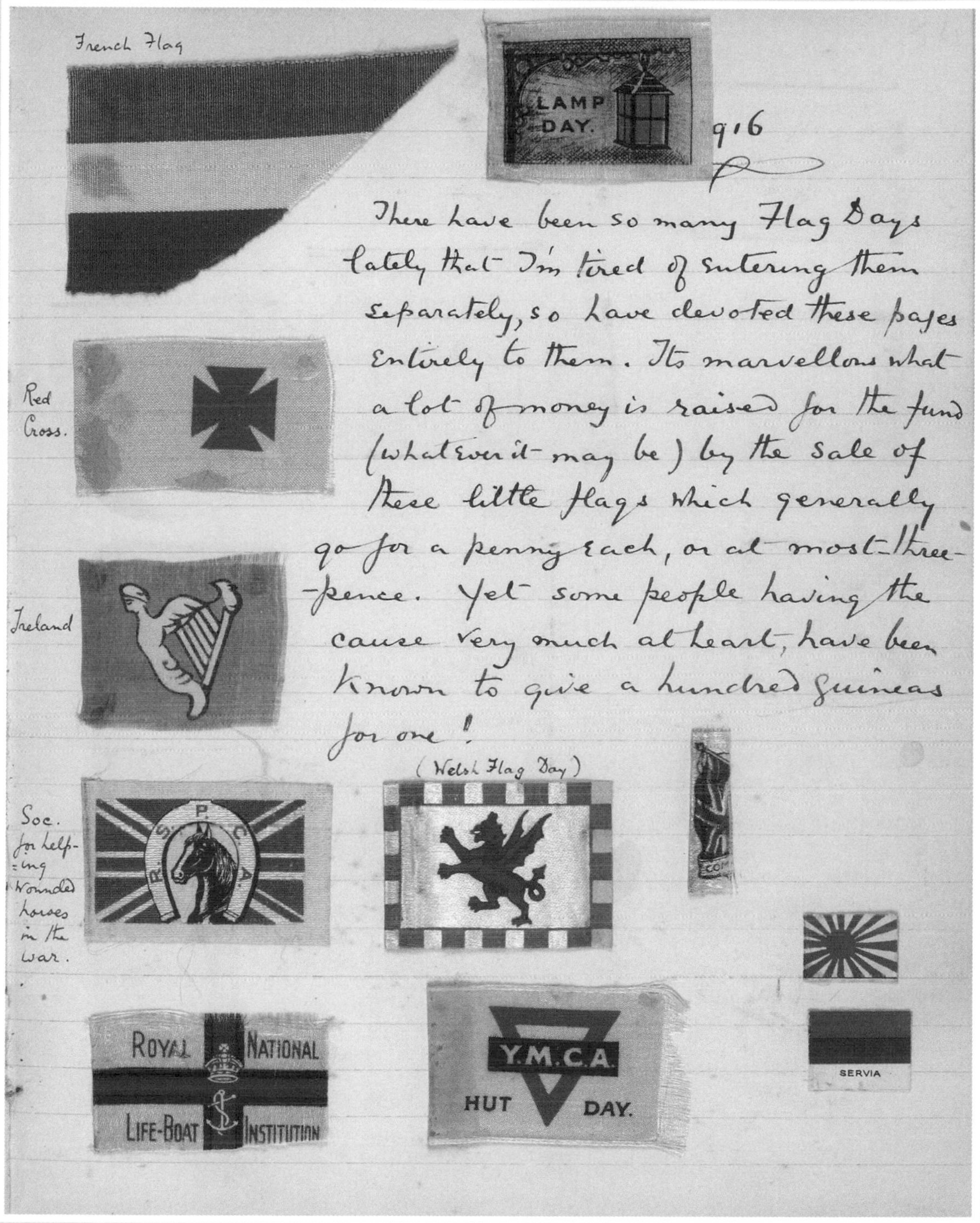

French Flag

LAMP DAY. 9·6

There have been so many Flag Days lately that I'm tired of entering them separately, so have devoted these pages entirely to them. Its marvellous what a lot of money is raised for the fund (whatever it may be) by the sale of these little flags which generally go for a penny each, or at most three-pence. Yet some people having the cause very much at heart, have been known to give a hundred guineas for one!

Red Cross.

Ireland

Soc. for help-ing Wounded horses in the war.

R.S.P.C.A.

(Welsh Flag Day)

ROYAL NATIONAL LIFE-BOAT INSTITUTION

Y.M.C.A. HUT DAY.

SERVIA

Dec. 14th 1916.

Another Christmas dawning! and yet no signs of
peace. The butchery and the carnage, and suffering
and death, continue with relentless fury. Men
seem to have lost all sense of manhood and
decency in their mad lust for blood.

Not only has the conflict been more deadly
than ever of late, but England has been torn with
political troubles at home. But a totally inefficient
government couldn't be allowed to go on, and
within the last few days great events have been
happening. Mr Asquith has discreetly(!!) resigned
and Lloyd George is now Prime Minister, and
has chosen an entirely new cabinet. He is a
man of actions (though I'd never trust a Welsh-
-man) and heaven knows the time has come
when we need action:— sharp, swift, and
decisive. For the last two years the
government has been prevaricating, & slack, &
for ever "putting off" or "waiting to see"!
Well, we shall see what the new Prime
Minister's tactics will be! I fancy we are
                    in for thrilling times at home!

—— 80 ——

## Friday 19th Jan. 1917.

So, the third year of the war has started, and as there is no sign whatever of its soon being over, I think I had better take to writing on both sides of the paper of this book, or it will mean another volume shortly!

*  *  *  *  *  *

Such an appalling disaster happened today, and as it is owing (indirectly) to this wicked awful war, — I must write about it in my war diary.

Last evening I was sitting alone over the fire, just dozing comfortably after a cold and cheerless day, when without any warning there came the most ghastly crashing explosion possible to imagine! Louder than the mightiest clap of thunder, I instantly made up my mind it was a german bomb that had been intended for Woolwich, but had dropped short and fallen on our lawn instead! The house shook, windows rattled, and so deafening and alarming was it that I sat rooted to my chair, breathlessly awaiting the next shock which one felt sure would follow.

But nothing happened, and then I tore upstairs

to look out of one of our upper windows which faces the direction of Woolwich, and sure enough the sky was all red and lurid and vibrating, & then I felt sure the arsenal was blown up and the whole of Woolwich in flames!!

No news came that night, but next day we heard that it was the most awful explosion of its kind ever known, as a munition factory in East London (at Silvertown) had caught fire somehow (ah! how?) and the fire spread till it reached all the explosives and then the whole place was hurled up into the air, and four streets were demolished, and the dead and the dying and the injured lay amongst the ruins, so that when a relief party arrived they hardly knew where to begin. A fire engine was twisted up into fragments, the unfortunate men being buried beneath. But endless are the stories of horror — unthinkable horrors — that are gradually coming to light.

When I heard that petrifying noise I knew something awful was going on somewhere, and that hundreds of lives were probably being given up. And they were.

Over a hundred people were killed, and more than four hundred injured and disabled.

## 4th February. 1917.

There is a saying that it is always "darkest before the dawn", and if that is true then the dawn ought not to be very far off! Certainly the present state of affairs could hardly be called "rosy". Germany's latest act of develry has been to issue a proclamation that she means to torpedo and sink every single ship, neutral or otherwise, that dares to show its face on the sea! This is to include hospital red cross ships, so that the poor unfortunate wounded are to be drowned like rats in a hole. Of course the whole world is in a ferment over such absolutely unparalled brutality. But Germany is now desperate, and thinks by stopping all our imported foodstuffs, to starve us out. Of course this last move is a very serious one for England in many ways, and already there is talk in the air of the country being put on equal food rations and tickets being distributed in order to get bread & meat. The war is coming very near home.....

April 1917.  Food is getting distinctly scarce
and one begins to feel as if we were living in the
days of the French Revolution! But a great deal
of nonsense is written by people saying we must
not think of giving even our crumbs to the poor birds.

Because we are fighting against
brutes must we ourselves become
brutes? Feeling strongly on the
matter I wrote to the Mirror this
letter, though from its extremely
flippant tone, I never expected
to see it in print!

We have not got compulsory
rations yet, but for the last four
Sundays, in every church and
chapel throughout the land, a
Proclamation from the King has
been read exhorting the people

**BUT DON'T WASTE THE CRUSTS!**

I CANNOT agree with "H. H. S." as regards "Birds and Bread." In these days, when everyone is living in supreme egotism as to how he or she may best reconcile the Food Controller with his or her own particular "little Mary," it is surely most refreshing to hear of certain lovers of animals who gladly spare a daily morsel for the birds.

Personally I thoroughly enjoy feeding them every morning with crusts and fragments of bread that would otherwise find their way into "the pig-tub"!

In theory it is excellent to say that "not a crust should now be wasted," but as a matter of fact in every well-to-do house stale remnants of bread are treated very much as they have always been treated, so why disappoint our little feathered friends who brighten this sombre world with their music, and at the same time free our precious crops from insect pests? — E. M. B.

to practise the most rigid economy, especially
in bread.  We are not allowed to feed our
horses on corn any longer and the poor dears are
growing dull and slack on hay! and dog
biscuits can no longer be got for love or money,
which is serious!

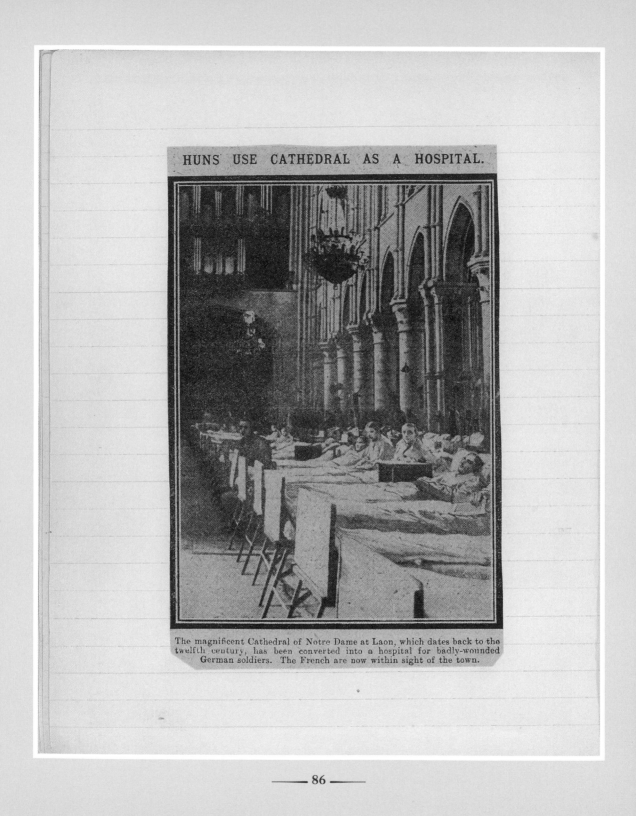

**HUNS USE CATHEDRAL AS A HOSPITAL.**

The magnificent Cathedral of Notre Dame at Laon, which dates back to the twelfth century, has been converted into a hospital for badly-wounded German soldiers. The French are now within sight of the town.

America has joined the fray! She couldn't well keep out of it any longer as the Germans have been calmly sinking her ships that came laden with grain to England; she certainly couldn't lay claim to her usual independence whilst that sort of thing went on. It will mean a big help to us, and a consignment of American nurses and surgeons have already arrived in England, and indeed we need them badly enough.

\* \* \* \* \*

When I began my war diary I thought it was great extravagance buying such a large book but as I intended writing only on one side of the pages, I thought the war might possibly stretch out as long enough to fill it with war incidents! But alas! the third year of war has come and there is no more sign of peace than when it first started, and I shall probably have to buy several diaries instead of one, and as paper is now ruinously dear, I must certainly write on both sides of a page in future. A friend from France writes "it seems to me we are in a dark tunnel, sans issue."

( Folkestone
Raid. )

Friday. May 25th. 1917.

The worst raid that we have experienced
(in England)
yet, took place in broad day light at 5.30.
Today, when sixteen hostile air craft
hovered over Folkestone, dropping bombs
in rapid succession. An awful scene followed.
People who were doing their Whitsuntide shopping
(for it's Whitsun week) were killed outright amidst
the falling débris of the shops; poor old
women, helpless children, babies in arms,
all were ruthlessly mutilated—killed and
wounded; for a bomb is no respecter of persons.
72 killed, & 114 seriously injured, — oh
brave noble cultured Germany!!!

Herbert Dale, our cousin who is vicar of
Hythe, — where twenty eight bombs were also
dropped, — was standing in the churchyard
with his wife talking to their Verger. The
latter suddenly pointed out a fleet
of aeroplanes sailing overhead— "out
for practise" he said, taking them to be
our men! The next minute the poor old
man fell killed, and Herbert &

his wife had a marvellous escape.

I wrote an account of Folkestone under the heading of "the Land we love" in the "National News", as the place is very much in the public eye just at present, and here is the small drawing I did of the old town taken from a pen & ink sketch done four or five years ago. But I hear these dear old houses are now no more.

A corner of old Folkestone.

(E.M. Bilbrough)

—(Lafayette.)

**The Bishop Stands By.**—Here is the bomb-defying Bishop, the Bishop of Dover, who, " as an expression of sympathy with the East Coast raid sufferers, has decided to sleep at Ramsgate on moonlight nights and share the anxiety of any possible alarms." Doubtless he had an opportunity of doing a considerable amount of anxiety-sharing in the early hours of yesterday morning. This is the right spirit for the clergy, and if more of them were to show it—well, I leave it at that. Dr. Bilborough, the Bishop, held many important ecclesiastical appointments in the North of England, and in his youth was a great footballer.

### FOLKESTONE AIR RAID.

#### VICAR'S NARROW ESCAPE.

Many sad stories were told at the adjourned inquest yesterday on victims of the Folkestone air raid, and the jury learnt, too, of marvellous escapes. The Vicar of Hythe, the Rev. Herbert Dixon Dale, had a terrible experience. A verger, Daniel Stringer Lyth, a man of 63, was among the dead.

The vicar, giving evidence, said the verger called his attention to aircraft passing overhead. Two bombs then fell, one eighty and another forty-five yards away. Lyth was standing between witness and his wife, and fell with a cry. Immediately after, the second bomb dropped. Witness's wife was struck by a fragment near the eye. Afterwards he found a piece of metal in his own pocket, which had penetrated the cloth and was stopped by a tin box, and he providentially escaped injury. Lyth was taken to hospital, where he died.

July 7th 1917.

A day when the war came "very near home" indeed.
I was peacefully at work on a pen & ink drawing
after breakfast — rather longing to be out in the
garden among the roses, for the sun was shining and
it was an ideal summers day, when presently the
whole air — the whole blue cloudless sky — seem'd
to become alive. Strange: uncanny sounds came from
the heights above, — untranslatable sounds, but
ominous and alarming in their uncertainty, and
then Ada put her head round the door saying
" I'm afraid there's an air raid on."; and I laid
down my pen with a sinking heart and understood.
        We assembled in the hall including "Jock," who
immediately
∧took the opportunity to go & have a good roll
                wet
on the ∧grass outside by slipping through the open
door! (he knows its forbidden!) but even if they
do love a good roll, dogs would never dream
of doing the dastardly actions the human
race are at present indulging in!
Well, there was no doubt there was a raid in
progress, & a pretty big one too. Over-head there
was a swarm of aeroplanes looking like

a flight of bees — or butterflies. But the noise! I shall
never forget it. There was the peculiar steady drone of
the ₍german₎ Engines, — loud enough, for they were very low down,
and then came the furious banging of the machine
guns showing that <u>our</u> aeroplanes had attacked the
enemy & were doing their best to bring some down.
Gracious heavens what next! a wild fight in the air
(thousands of feet above the earth) — in things like fearful
₍distorted₎ mechanical birds (only with no beauty,) which were
circling round each other & engaged in deadly combat;
dodging - swerving, diving and soaring, while sometimes
they would be lost sight of in a cloud of smoke. There was nothing
to be done; I didn't feel like going down into the cellar which
people say is the safest place, but I d<u>id</u> feel sick with
anxiety for I knew quite well so many squadrons would <u>only</u>
be sent over for one purpose, — an attack on London; (the last
on June 13th occurred when we were away,) & K's office is in the
heart of the city. As we were all watching this weird
& unnatural fight going on over head there was suddenly
a deafening bang quite close that made ones heart
jump; and some one said "That's <u>a bomb</u>!" — but it
wasn't; it was the big canon at Grove Park which
has never been let off before. I think they fired it two

or three times, and I thought Every moment the house would be struck by falling shrapnel or a bomb, for it was all very close at hand. It seem'd hours before they passed on in their mad flight and fight; in reality it must have been only about ten minutes before the sounds gradually diminished and then ceased altogether. And one looked round half dazed on a world that was still beautiful and peaceful and sunny, and wondered if it had all been a hideous night=mare?. Then the thought of London returned in full force, and the next half hour of gnawing fear & anxiety I shall remember to my dying day. An awful feeling of helplessness was dominant; telephones would be "off", telegraphs all stopped, how could I find out if all was well? and then a blessed boy appeared from our neighbour's with a telephone message, — I will give the actual one as a memento of a very horrible morning when the "great war reached Chislehurst! or rather the City.

[only about 200 yards from Ken's Office.

[Three bombs fell within a few yards of each other in Fenchurch-street in this first daylight raid. One five-floor block of offices was practically demolished: here 19 people were killed and five injured.

Air raid in the city Mr Kenneth all right.

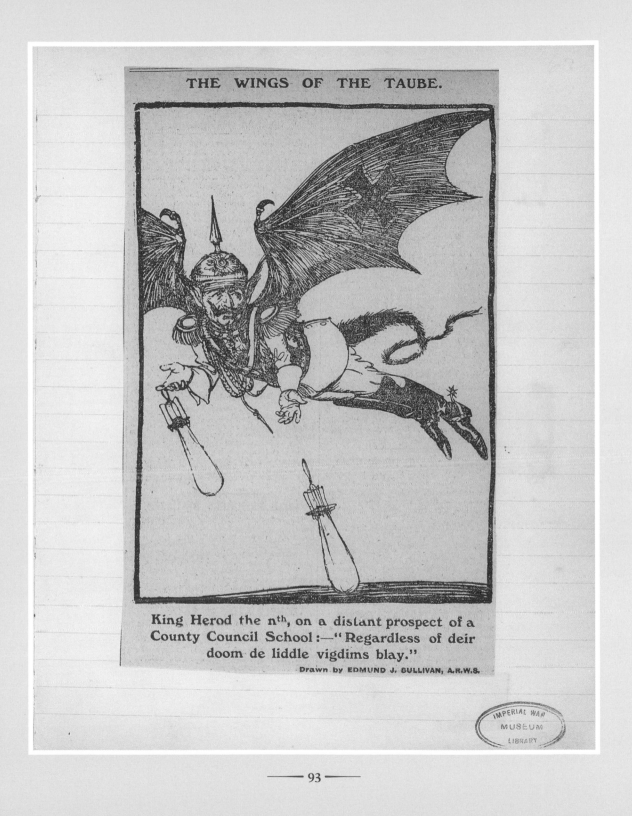

THE WINGS OF THE TAUBE.

King Herod the nth, on a distant prospect of a County Council School:—"Regardless of deir doom de liddle vigdims blay."

Drawn by EDMUND J. SULLIVAN, A.R.W.S.

Flag Day for building Sailors & Soldiers Club!

November 4th 1917.

Poor old England is going through dark days
just now, and one cannot see the faintest prospect
of peace in sight. Russia has failed us when we
most needed her help, and her armies have ignominiously
retreated, covered with shame instead of glory,
and now the news comes that our other ally —
Italy — has suffered a terrible defeat at the hands
of the Huns, and two hundred thousand Italians
have been taken prisoners.      In the mean while
the inhuman barbarians who go by the name
of Germans, continue to send their Gothas and
their Zepplins by stealth in the dead of night —
to drop their vindictive bombs on unfortunate
civilians in London and the Suburbs. The cowardly
wickedness of such raids is almost incredible;
to think of defenceless innocent women and
children, and old men and boys being ruthlessly
murdered and mutilated by these devils in
the air is unspeakably horrible. But as
some one said the other day, "There are no
civilians now, we are all soldiers." Still,
soldiers have the power to hit back, but what
chance have poor frightened folk in their beds?

The odious U boats continue to wreck and torpedo every vessel on the seas, and the number of ships and steamers that go to the bottom every week is appalling, especially when one remembers that many of them are bringing food stuffs to England. The awful wholesale waste of it all! the fishes are having the time of their lives! and we poor Britishers have to pay the penalty in practising the most rigid economy at our tables! The extraordinary thing is that we arn't at the point of starvation!

Prices of course are awful, here is a little list that shows how enormously things have risen in cost since the war began.—

Nov. 2ⁿᵈ 1917.

Yesterday I wanted to buy a small tinned tongue which formerly cost about 2/— to my consternation the man demanded 4/6 !!

I walked straight out of the shop with <u>no</u> tongue beyond what nature has blessed me with gratuitously !, & used it freely !

Once again Ken has been collecting for St
Dunstans, and this
year he has far sur-
-passed his fine total
of last year as will be
seen by the account
here given. Moreover
Queen Alexandra also
wrote him a personal
letter of thanks, which
was extremely nice of
her, for its not every one
who can claim the
distinction of having
received a letter of
gratitude from a Queen!
and written in her
own hand writing, not
even typed, which makes
a great difference. There
is something so character-
=isticless about a type-written
letter somehow, it has come from a machine
instead of a living being —.

## ST. DUNSTAN'S HOSTEL FOR BLINDED HEROES.

### QUEEN ALEXANDRA'S LETTER TO MR. KENNETH BILBROUGH.

Her Majesty Queen Alexandra, as Patroness of St. Dunstan's Hostel for Blinded Soldiers and Sailors, has personally written a letter of thanks to Mr. Kenneth L Bilbrough, a Member of Lloyd's and an old school-fellow of Sir Arthur Pearson, expressing her very appreciative thanks for his work on behalf of the funds of St. Dunstan's.

The text of the letter, which was in her Majesty's own handwriting, is as follows:—

Sandringham,
Sept. 18, 1917.

Dear Mr. Bilbrough,

I have just heard from Sir Arthur Pearson of the truly magnificent sum of £60,000 which you have personally collected and have given to him for the present and after-care of our poor blinded soldiers and sailors, in whose behalf I am so deeply interested.

I wish to express to you my heartfelt and grateful thanks for your splendid effort on behalf of these heroes of the war, and I am proud to be the Patroness of St. Dunstan's Home, where they are so tenderly cared for and looked after by Sir Arthur Pearson, and which has now, owing to you, been so magnificently assisted in its great work.

Believe me,
Yours sincerely,
(Signed) ALEXANDRA.

The splendid sum of £67,000 has been raised in the course of two years through Mr. Bilbrough's systematic appeals to individuals and firms in the shipping, insurance, banking and commercial world, the amount in the first year aggregating £15,000.

This year Mr. Bilbrough made a further appeal for the men of St. Dunstan's, which met with a response even more liberal than the very generous one accorded to him before. A noteworthy addition to the present year's list of donors is found in the names of the two Archbishops and 34 of our Bishops, who have readily responded to and personally signed Mr. Bilbrough's appeal. Altogether Mr. Bilbrough has personally collected nearly £57,000 for the benefit of those heroes who have made so tremendous a sacrifice for the cause of their country and their Allies. Furthermore, by arousing the sympathy of influential friends he has been instrumental in securing an additional sum of about £10,000 for the funds, thereby making a total of £67,000—an achievement upon which he is to be heartily congratulated.

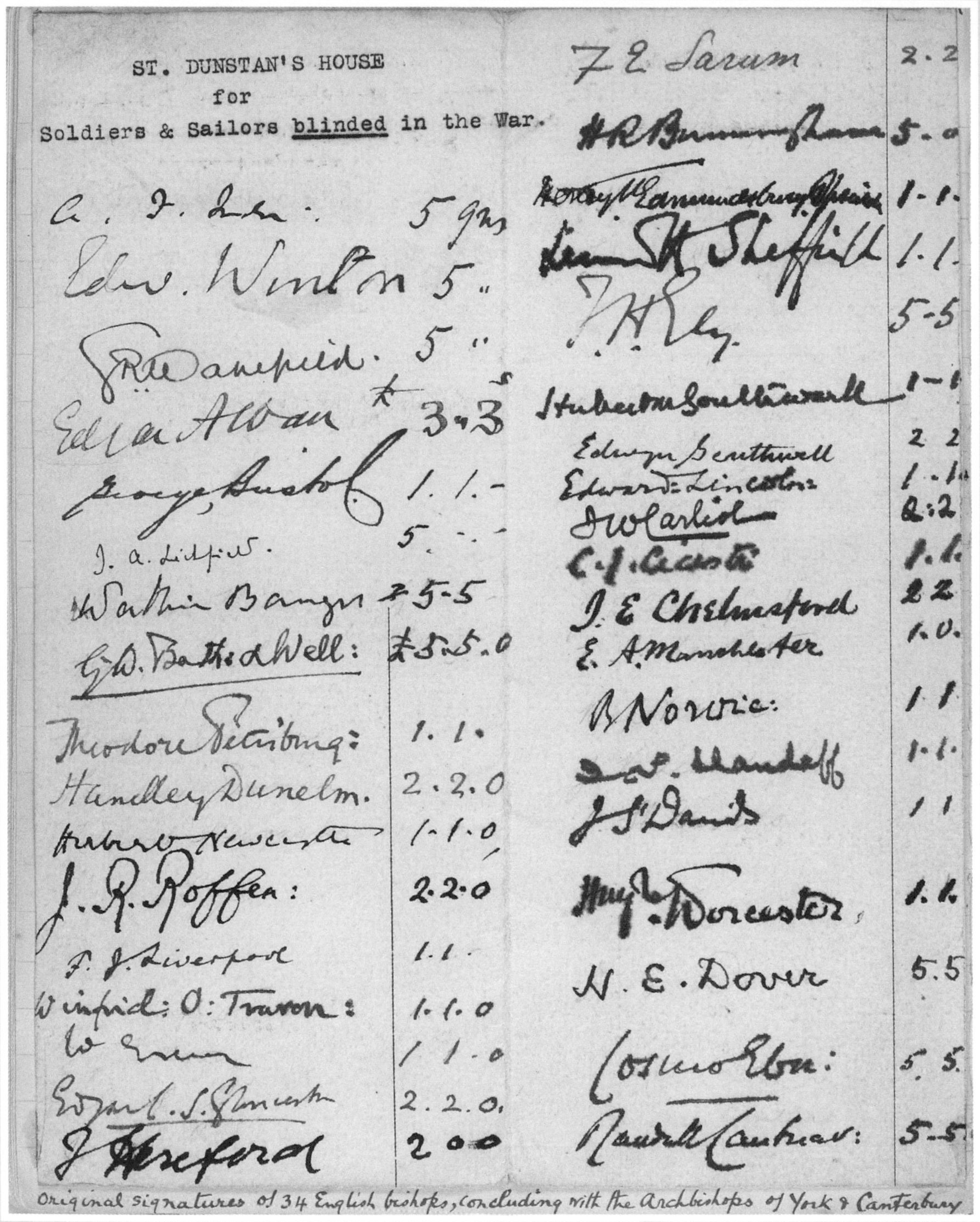

ST. DUNSTAN'S HOUSE
for
Soldiers & Sailors blinded in the War.

| | |
|---|---|
| [illegible] | 5 gns |
| Edw. Winton | 5 " |
| [illegible] | 5 " |
| Edgar Alban | £3-3-5 |
| George, Bristol | 1. 1. - |
| J. A. Lichfield | 5. - - |
| Watkin Bangor | £5-5 |
| G. W. Bath & Well: | £5-5-0 |
| Theodore Petriburg: | 1. 1. |
| Handley Dunelm. | 2. 2. 0 |
| Hubert Newcastle | 1-1-0 |
| J. R. Roffen: | 2-2-0 |
| F. J. Liverpool | 1.1. |
| Winfrid: O: Truron: | 1-1-0 |
| [illegible] | 1 1-0 |
| Edgar C. S. Glouceste | 2. 2. 0. |
| J. Hereford | 2 0 0 |

| | |
|---|---|
| F. E. Sarum | 2. 2 |
| H. R. Bury[illegible] | 5. 0 |
| [illegible] | 1-1- |
| [illegible] Sheffield | 1. 1- |
| F. H. Ely. | 5-5 |
| Hubert M. Southwark | 1-1 |
| Edwyn Southwell | 2 2 |
| Edward: Lincoln: | 1. 1. |
| J. W. Carliol | 2:2 |
| C. J. Leicester | 1. 1. |
| J. E. Chelmsford | 2 2 |
| E. A. Manchester | 1. 0. |
| B. Norvic: | 1 1 |
| [illegible] Llandaff | 1. 1. |
| J. St. Davids | 1 1 |
| Hugh [illegible] Worcester | 1. 1. |
| H. E. Dover | 5. 5 |
| Cosmo Ebor: | 5. 5. |
| Randall Cantuar: | 5-5 |

Original signatures of 34 English bishops, concluding with the Archbishops of York & Canterbury

# BLINDED SOLDIERS' AND SAILORS' HOSTEL.

## 29887

St. Dunstan's,

Regent's Park, N.W.

28ᵗʰ November 1917

Received from K. Bilbrough Esq

the sum of Fiftyseven thousand Pounds nine Shillings

and seventy four Pence.

£57074 : 9 : —

Arthur Pearson

Original receipt for fifty seven thousand pounds (collected by
K. L. Bilbrough) & signed by Sir Arthur Pearson (first instalment
only.)

## November 1917.

Two bad reverses have befallen the Allies this month, the worst being the total collapse of Russia, which, consumed by revolution and anarchy, has broken its treaty and turned traitor to the Allies, offering a separate peace to Germany. This is a blow, as it will liberate all the german soldiers kept in Russia now, who will return to reinforce their regiments at the front. One has no words for Russia, her mean cowardly conduct is unspeakable.

Then Italy. For a long while no one heard much about Italy, and then quite suddenly the Italians started retreating, in other words running away!, or throwing up their hands as a sign of capitulation. And so we and the French have had to send whole armies to help them when all the time we need every single man we have to help in France.

Oh this war! will the end of it ever come? peace seems farther off than ever, and our men freeze in the bitter cold of the

trenches and the flower of our land is getting
ruthlessly slain and slaughtered day by day:
— oh the pity of it all, the wicked waste of
fresh young lives, and the misery and
wreckage their deaths leave in thousands
of broken hearts, to whom nothing will ever be the same
again. It is terrible to see how lengthy the list
grows in the little war shrine at church (even in
a small place like this) for those who have laid
down their lives for King and country.
And it is hard for those left who still struggle
bravely on, to put Patriotism before Peace.
But a peace now would not be an honourable
one or a lasting one, because were a treaty
even possible, we know by past experience that
Germany has no respect for either treaties or
honour.        But how in Heaven's name
will it all end? and when?

LEAGUE OF NATIONAL SAFETY

I gladly enrol you as a member of this League.

*Arthur K. Yapp.*

Director of Food Economy
Grosvenor House.
London. W.1.

From Sir Arthur Yapp,
(to me!)

LNS. 2.

FOOD ECONOMY
NATIONAL SAFETY

PLEASE ENROL MY NAME [...]
OF NATIONAL SAFETY. I REALIZE TH[...]
IN THE USE OF ALL FOOD AND THE CHECKING [...]
WASTE HELPS MY COUNTRY TO COMPLETE VICTORY.[...]
I PROMISE TO ABIDE BY THE NEW SCALE OF VOLUNTARY
RATIONS AND TO DO ALL IN MY POWER TO ASSIST THIS
CAMPAIGN FOR NATIONAL SAFETY.

NAME (capitals)    Ethel M Belbrough
(Mr., Mrs. or Miss.)

ADDRESS (capitals)    Elmstead Grange
                      Chislehurst.

NO MEMBERSHIP FEES.
ANYONE OVER SIXTEEN YEARS OF AGE MAY JOIN.

SIGN AND POST THIS CARD. NO STAMPS NEEDED.

COUNTY _____

BADGE WILL BE SENT FREE IN DUE COURSE

One card only to be signed by each person.

"League of National Safety", of which I have just
become a member! The object of the league
is voluntary economy & rationing.

January 1918.

The Christmas of 1917 has come and gone, and we have now entered upon our fourth year of war. One feels thankful that the old year has departed, & no-one will ever look back on 1917 without a thrill of horror.  The King and Queen have sent such nice messages at this time to the Empires fighters, that I give it word for word.

I send to all ranks of the Navy and Army my hearty good wishes for Christmas and the New Year.

I realise your hardships, patiently and cheerfully borne, and rejoice in the successes you have won so nobly.

The nation stands faithful to its pledges, resolute to fulfil them

May God bless your efforts and give us victory.  GEORGE R.I.

Our Christmas thoughts are with the sick and wounded sailors and soldiers. We know by personal experience with what patience and cheerfulness their suffering is borne.

We wish all a speedy restoration to health, a restful Christmastide and brighter days to come.  GEORGE R.I.
MARY R.

Poor King George! he must often feel he would gladly change places with any irresponsible crossing sweeper in the land! No English King has ever found himself in such an awful world-wide struggle before. —

One wonders what the new year 1918 will bring? — it is bound to be a year of crisis, for food supplies are running short and the enemy that we shall all have to fight before very long will be famine & starvation if the present state of things continue. And yet every day

more and more ships are sunk by the dastardly
U boats, and millions of tons of priceless
foodstuffs go to the bottom of the sea.

Meat is getting scarce and we have had no
butter or margarine for a fortnight! I am rather
glad, because when one is struggling with a slice
of horrid dry toast that rebels against going down,
one really feels one is at last taking part in the
war!! How poor people live is a mystery! for
fish is ruinous, and in a little Kentish village at Xmas
rabbits were being sold for 6/ and 10/ apiece!!
And now this week one reads in the paper of
a fowl going for 15/!! Worst of all, the English-
-man's standby, — bacon— is unprocurable!

But all this is vastly insignificant in comparison
to air raids, which every one lives in terror of
when the moon gets full! I hate to see that
bright white light at night, for with it one
expects every moment to hear the horrible
sound of engines overhead, & the booming of
great guns close at hand — ugh!

# Jan. 19th 1918.

This morning I was somewhat nonplussed by Ada bringing me the information that the butcher had come but had **no** meat for our lunch! As it was then past twelve, things didn't look promising, moreover being a Saturday the "cupboard was bare" — as it usually is at the end of the week. I had to dress hurriedly, catch up a basket, and depart for the village in order to forage for a meal. Mercifully fowls still produce eggs though butchers have ceased to produce meat,! and they (the fowls) didn't fail me. But it looks ominous, for the future, and things are getting harder & harder—especially for the poor, and I think it's Exasperating of Lord Rhonda to calmly accuse the people of being "greedy growsers" (his own words) when there's no meat, & precious little fish, (& that a prohibitive price,) & no cheese, nor bacon, nor butter, nor margarine nor marmalade, nor jam, nor sugar! "greedy growsers"! indeed!: Like that silly statesman — (I forget his name) who, after some horrible air raid in which several people were killed & mutilated & injured, accused the multitude of being a set of "Squealing Jays"!! I never hear a harsh voiced jay now (and we have several about our garden,) without thinking of the imbecility of
government officials!!

Jan. 23rd 1918

If it wern't for all the horrors of this awful war, the present situation here at home might certainly be said to have its humorous side! The idea of our stolid British householders having to forego their everlasting Sunday joint—" (which hiterto has been regarded as unalterable as the law of gravity!) and to do without butter, and to sit down to a baconless breakfast, is all really very comic. There's one thing an Englishman (or woman) does not shine at, and that is in adapting themselves to changed circumstances. We are all hugely conservative, and imagine that the things which have become habitual are equally unchangeable. The butchers shops have all been closed now for four days, and its said there is no prospect of their opening again for a considerable time, which is not to be wondered at as they can get no meat at the markets! Yesterday we had'nt a morsel of bread in the house, & I had to order the carriage & go & fetch, & bring home the loaves myself! Lean people will turn into skeletons at this rate, & fat people will get quite good figures!!

Monday 28th Jan. 1918.

It is twelve o'clock at night! A strange hour to be writing in a diary, but we are sitting up — Ken and I — after a most horrible air-raid, waiting for the "all clear" signal to go (which it won't do), and yet there have been no guns for over an hour. And we are waiting, too, for Puncher's return — who is a special constable, — and who always gets back soon after all is quiet. The firing began to night just as we were finishing dinner, the sickening "ping — g — g'''" that one knows so well! sounded just as I was starting on an apple (that never got eaten!) And then it all went on intermittantly for about two hours and a half, and at 9.30. the noise was awful! the barage sounded as if it was on our lawn, & we saw the shells breaking up in the sky just like shattered stars, — (unpleasantly near.)

We are getting dreadfully sleepy with the horrid wakeful sleepiness that follows some great mental excitement. Ten minutes past twelve!! Why doesn't Puncher come? Ken puts on more coals, and I tried to knit, but dropped so many stitches I soon threw it aside. —

(Next day) I had to give up writing here as it was

getting decidedly cold, and we drew up our chairs to the fire and watched the clock. Twelve thirty came; we were utterly mystified; and then through the silence rang out a quick bang-bang — horribly loud and like a sort of bark! One's heart sank! They were coming back! — it was all about to recommence, when we were dead with sleep, & chilled all through. The "barking" continued, & the great window on the stairs shook all over, and so did the front-door (& so did I!) We understood at last why the "all clear" bugle had not been sounded, and why Puncher had not returned.

Firing continued, and at 1.15. Ada came in with some hot tea!, and then at 1.30. we heard — oh! so thankfully — the "all clear" signal sound, and, tired and raid-racked! we toiled up to bed, where I lay till morning wide awake, and thinking of all the horrors those fiendish Gothas' had accomplished in their hellish night's work.

The papers said 58 were killed and about 200 injured, but they keep things back, and all the raid news is now suppressed. But many terrible things happened (in London,) amongst others a panic took place in one of the tube shelters and fourteen people (including seven children) were trampled to death. A bomb struck a high building where there were huge water tanks which crashed straight down into the cellars, where thirty people had taken refuge. They were all killed, and most of them were drowned.

Apart from any personal fear during these hateful raids, one cannot help feeling <u>sick</u> with apprehension as to what is going on [assuredly] <u>some</u> where all the while, while one listens to the incessant booming of the guns, sometimes near at hand, sometimes far off. And for nights afterwards, the sound seems to recur, and it eats into one's brain in the still hours of the night, however much one may fight against it. A powerful imagination is a tiresome thing to have! but its temperamental (if there's such a word!) and sometimes it helps one to picture <u>nice</u> things very vividly, so on the whole it has its compensations, like everything else.

The fierce "starlight raid" which took place on the night of Thurs.7th Mar, brought the horrors of it very near home, for a bomb was dropped almost within a stone's throw of my brother's house in Randolph Crescent. No one was in the least expecting a raid as there was no moon, only bright starlight, and every one was more or less astounded when the maroons went off soon after eleven. As an "eye witnesse's" account of a thing is always more interesting (and more reliable) than an outsider's, I will quote word for word from my brother's letter the day after the raid. — He writes thus. "Thank God we are all alive! but "it has been a near thing. We got the "warning" at 11.20, and " "went down into the basement; the guns had only just " "started when there was the most appallingly awful crash " "that it is possible to describe. Lilian was hit on the head " "by a bit of plaster but mercifully it was nothing serious, " "& they were all very brave. The houses struck (just " "the other side of the gardens) are gone, and every home " "in the crescent is wrecked. After the "all clear" had " "gone I recollect forcing back the billiard room door " "(smashed off its hinges, & piled with débris) and then we " "saw that awful sight of the houses across the garden all

"on fire, and reduced to ruins, many poor imprisoned "
"people being below and powerless to get out, and I "
"shall never forget their heart rending screams to my dying "
"day. All night long hundreds of rescuers were working "
"furiously, but it was over 15 hours before many bodies "
"could be recovered. Our vicar worked magnificently "
"and so did a local doctor who managed to pump oxygen "
"down a pipe to those who were being suffocated by the "
"heaps of debris beneath which they were buried"........//

This from the pen of one's own brother makes
one realise things far more than reading it
frome some newspaper's account, which are rarely
reliable. Of course the raid left their home
uninhabitable, and they have migrated to a peaceful
riverside residence in the Thames Valley, and I dont
think, after such a ghastly experience, they will ever
care to spend another night in London while the
war lasts. [ N.B. "To come very near death, teaches
one to value life .]

# Good Friday.
### 29th March 1918.

The last ghastly and inhuman act the Germans have perpetrated has been the shelling of a church in Paris (on Good Friday) which was filled with people taking part in the most sacred and the most solemn service of the year.

The Huns have just introduced a new abomination in the shape of a long range gun — or "mystery gun" as it goes by the name of here — which can fire its shells 80 or 90 miles. And they are bombarding Paris daily, & if they got to Calais, they would turn it on to London.

Dr. Fritz Rauserberger, who, it is stated, is the designer of the long-range gun which has been shelling Paris

( Note his horrible "long-range" head !! )

## LONG-RANGE GUN TRAGEDY.

### PARIS CHURCH STRUCK BY SHELL. during Good Friday

### 75 WORSHIPPERS KILLED.

PARIS, Saturday.

A shell fired by the German long-range gun struck a church in the Paris district during a Good Friday service. Seventy-five of the congregation were killed and ninety were wounded, including a great number of women and children. Among those killed were M. Stroehling, Councillor of the Swiss Legation, and Madame Stroehling, Brigadier-General Francfort, of the Reserves, Dr. Delouvrier, Dr. Mendelssohn, Count Jean Maussion and Miss Coningham.

It was about 4 p.m. that a violent detonation was heard. The shell smashed through the vaulted roof, making a breach of from five to six square yards. A mass of stones and brickwork was sent flying into the nave, crushing a great number of persons.

**SCENES OF DESTRUCTION.**

The frightful noise caused by the bursting of the shell shook the church to its foundations, causing a large portion of the arches and the left side of the nave to collapse. Cries of horror from the terror-stricken worshippers filled the church. The shell struck one of the large pillars between the windows which sustain the roof, causing it to collapse, and bringing the arch down. Stones and heavy material came down from a height of sixty feet, falling on the congregation. Splinters and portions of the exploded shell flew about in all directions. Some fragments of the metal struck the walls of the nave and the organ and ricocheted to the choir stalls.

By 5 p.m. close on sixty wounded victims had been taken to hospital and forty corpses removed from the ruins. These figures grew as helpers continued to search amongst the debris, and finally numbered seventy-five dead and ninety injured. When President Poincaré arrived there were already present the Prefect of Police and Cardinal Amette, the Archbishop of Paris, who stood gazing with eyes filled with tears at the terrible spectacle which confronted them.

"The wretches—the wretches," cried the Archbishop, "they have chosen the day and the hour Christ died on the Cross to commit this crime."

The Abbé of the church stated in an interview that a sacred concert was about to be given in the church, where the choristers were already assembled. When the first notes of the organ pealed out the church was crowded. Suddenly the brutal crime was perpetrated. "It is horrible," commented the Abbé, "and I still ask myself if I am not suffering from some ghastly nightmare."—Exchange.

"From National News "(Easter Sunday)

## Easter, 30th March, 1918.

The "great push" by the Germans on the Western front which Everyone has been feverishly ~waiting~ for, has commenced at last, and the Huns in appalling numbers are hurling themselves on our lines, mad to break through. Never has there been a more anxious or critical time in the whole war, and we daily hold our breath for news. Our poor brave boys are far outweighed in numbers by the Germans who have Endless fresh divisions always coming up, and it is three to one. Already they have forced us back, but the allies are making a fine stand inspite of the heavy odds against them.

## THE RUINED CRECHE—KULTUR'S LATEST TRIUMPH!

Last Friday, during the bombardment of Paris by the long-range gun, one of the shells struck a crèche, with the result that four persons were killed and twenty-one wounded. The wrecked dormitory, showing where the shell entered.

Lord Rhonda, the great Food Controller, has just died. Poor man! he had rationed himself too severely, and when he got ill with pleurisy or something, he had no strength left to fight against it. But he will be much missed, for he worked out the appalling problem of placing England under food rations with amazing skill and foresight. It was he who introduced the ration cards which every soul has had: no one could get any meat or butter or bacon or poultry without presenting in exchange an absurd little paper coupon. Neither at a restaurant nor an hotel may one procure meat without one, though "a half portion" is permitted, in which case the coupon is divided! In years to come people will hardly believe that such things really <u>were</u>, and yet they not only exist at the present day, but the whole scheme has succeeded wonderfully well, in spite of the stupendous difficulties that had to be overcome. Here is a genuine meat "coupon" of the Great War! (some people always call them "Kupongs"!) It would buy meat to the value of <u>fivepence</u> only, & each person is allowed three meat coupons per week, so we don't get fat on <u>that</u>!

18

Why in the world should we adopt the french word "coupon" I wonder? and the funny thing is that the french have adopted an english one for the same thing, & talk about their "teekets"!

———————

Things look about as gloomy as they possibly can. The sinking of our ships (daily) by the German submarines, continues in appalling numbers. The pent-up fury of the Huns is all being concentrated in their last "Great Offensive", and — our lines are broken badly at the front, yet our brave boys remain undaunted, and continue the struggle valiantly against tremendous odds.      I keep thinking of Watts picture of "Hope"; it is strangely applicable to the present time ......  We may be downcast, (and certainly are,) but there is always that deathless string of "Hope" left, though all else seems shattered and tottering.       Fortunately the thought of England conquered is unthinkable, — (which sounds rather a paradox!)
      The Kaiser has (with his usual humility(?) announced his intention of completely "crushing" the British Army!

(See opposite page.) Hole on Pauls Cray Common (and now filled with water,) which was caused by a bomb from Enemy aircraft overhead, on the night of May 19th, 1918, during a raid.

Spring 1918. (June)

The weather is nearly as depressing as the war news; the rain and the cold chill one, as does the fact that the Germans are gradually but steadily pushing nearer to Paris day by day. This unfortunate city is much worse off than London, for it is relentlessly shelled by "Big Bertha" (the long range gun) during the day, and bombed by relays of Gothas during the night!

The last London raid occurred on May 19th, but thank goodness we were many miles away, safe in peaceful Glastonbury! It began at eleven at night and was one of the worst raids we[?] have experienced; nearly fifty people were killed and over 161 injured. Chislehurst too came in for some bombing on this occasion, one bomb was dropped on Pauls Cray Common, and another just outside the Parish Church, which mercifully fell in the grass of the common, and did no damage beyond breaking the windows all round, and making a large hole in the Common, not quite as big as its rival excavation the Cockpit, old which is only a few feet away!!

It makes the war seem horribly real when when these nerve-shattering bombs are dropped at one's very door! (see opposite.)

June 4$\underline{th}$

The postage rate has now been increased as a means of extra taxation, and from today no more letters will be sent for a penny. They will all be three halfpence, and post cards will be 1$^d$ instead of a $\frac{1}{2}^d$.            [Shan't write so many letters in future!]

June 14ᵗʰ

This morning we were all busy at the hospital
depôt helping to make such queer garments. They
are intended for our Snipers at the front, and are
like great shapeless bags of coarse linen canvas.
When they are stitched together, they go to London,
where they are painted by various artists all sorts
of colours representing earth, twigs, and grass,
in order to mystify and decieve the enemy. The
Snipers also wear helmets with tufts of grass and moss
stuck into them, and, when they are completely turned
out, what horrid uncanny looking objects they must
be!, creeping stealthily along the enemies lines under
cover of the darkness.

\*     \*     \*     \*     \*     \*

Thank goodness America has at length intervened
and is now drawn in to this vast world-wide
struggle, and not a moment too soon, for even the
cheeriest optimists have been going about with long
faces lately, and we have hardly dared to look ahead.
    But now this great country has come to the aid of
the allies, — and also to preserve her own shipping,
which the Germans have been ruthlessly distroying by
their U boats, when it came in their way, — but now
WE SHALL SEE !!

## Sunday, 4th August. 1918.

A lovely day which was fortunate, as being the fourth anniversary of the war, a special form of service has been drawn up to be held throughout the land, and our's took place in the old cock-pit on the common!! Truly the war has worked wonders! and conventionalities are no longer regarded as they were. The service was held by the Rector, the Vicar, and the Wesleyan minister! who wisely forgot their doctrinal differences, and agreed to meet as fellow christians & brothers, thinking of nothing but the wide-spread need of prayer just now for every-one, apart from any sect or (creed.) The cock-pit was filled to over-flowing with a very great & well behaved congregation who extended over a greater part of the common as well. The three clerics were all in plain white surplices — (which looked queer blowing about in the wind, — !) the rector and vicar had abandoned stoles and cassocks and birettas & other ritual garments, while the Wesleyan minister had consented to put on a white surplice for the first time in his life!! It was a very impressive service, held under the blue sky of heaven, and once an aeroplane flew low, right over our very heads, and I couldn't help thinking "Suppose its an enemy one, come to drop bombs on this vast concourse of people"!! But nothing happened, and even the rain kept off, which would have been nothing short of a calamity as no one had brought umbrellas in spite of some rather ominous thunder clouds hanging about.

The Rector opened the service by reading the following; and all the people kept so quiet you could have heard a pin drop. "Brethren, on this fourth aniversary of the "declaration of War, let us draw near to God in "penitence and humility; let us pray Him to de-"-liver us from the temptations that beset us, and if "it be His Will, to grant us victory and peace. "Let us implore His help for all those who are "engaged at home or abroad in carrying on the "war; and let us thank Him for mercies already "vouchsafed to us." Then followed a special litany and prayers, and a few well known hymns like "Oh God our help in Ages past" and "Holy Father in Thy Keeping" & others, and then we

all walked home to tea in a suitable and
orderly manner! Its a pity we don't have
more out of door services, the people like them
and behave well, but of course there's always
the danger of a few black sheep being about
and causing disturbances, and the uncertainty of
our English climate is a drawback which cannot be
overcome.

July 16<sup>th</sup> 1918.

The Germans have begun their <u>third</u> great Offensive,
and thank Heaven the Allies are holding their own,
and in some cases we have even driven the Enemy
back. ‖    The poor dethroned Tzar of Russia
has just been shot, and all Russia is in a state
of frenzied revolution and disorder.

August.

Things begin to look Ever so much brighter
than they did, and Every one is going about
with a much lighter step and a much lighter
heart. Several towns which we lost in the last
Offensive, such as Soissons, Bapaume, and
Péronne, have all been regained. In one's
own imagination one is inclined to think of these
places as still intact, but an interesting letter
from a friend in France * throws light on
this subject. He writes — "The desolation of "
" Northern France is simply indescribable. An "
" absolutely dead world, with no signs of life any‑"
"‑where. Miles upon miles of dead trees, not a "
" village to be seen, for they are all gone. There is "
" literally not a trace of all those villages & towns "

* Col. H. Fortesue.

" the names of which you read of daily in the papers "
" as being "retaken". Bapaume, Péronne, &c are "
" a mere heap of stones. Arras is a complete ruin, "
" not a single house left habitable. Amiens has "
" suffered a good deal of damage, particularly "
" in the principal street and round the Cathedral — "
" which by some extraordinary coincidence has "
" practically remained uninjured. The only "
" damage I could see to it, was where one field gun "
" shell had fallen through the roof, to become em= "
" =bedded in the pavement of the nave beneath " ......

### October 1918

This has been a most eventful month, and it seems impossible to believe that the End is in sight at last. Is it really true that after these four interminable years of uphill fighting and grappling against tremendous odds, that we are finally going to win?. No Englishman would ever admit it, not even to himself, but I believe there have been times in the war when the paralysing thought has flashed through our minds that we were going to get — well, that we were not going to win!

But now all is changed. America's timely help came just when it was most needed, and it also inspired the allies to buck up and fight with redoubled zeal and deathless courage.

At the beginning of the month Bulgaria caved in, and on the 28th Austria (who has been getting dreadfully tired of fighting for a long while past;) pleaded desperately for a separate peace.

Turkey was the next enemy to throw up the sponge, and on the 31st of this month an armistice was signed between us.

So, taking it all round, its been a wonderful month, and

now the whole world is watching with breathless interest the moves of President Wilson and the great Field Marshal, Foch, — who is a fine frenchman. After all, military manoevres very much resemble a complicated game of chess, — only the pawns are living souls unhappily!

President Wilson.

Mr. Wilson, who is expected to land in France on Thursday and will afterwards visit England. He is the first American President to visit Europe whilst in office.—*Stanley.*

Marshal Foch.

Marshal Foch, who, as supreme commander of the Allies forces, announces armistice terms to German envoys.

We must salute also the great general, Marshal Foch, to whom, more than to any living man, we owe it that to-day—instead of to-morrow, instead of months and years hence—the nightmare is lifted from our minds.

Sunday Evening. 10th Nov. 1918.

# KAISER ABDICATES :

The above startling words appeared in this morn-ing's Sunday paper, and needless to say, they have thrown us all into a state of thrilling expectancy and pent-up excitement. A report was also circulated that the Armistice between Germany & the Allies had been signed! — which would of course mean the end of hostilities and — peace! But there was nothing authentic to go by, and the day passed with no further reliable news, though the Kaiser's Abdication (which is official) is good enough news for one day! And that little worm—the crown prince—has also made a bolt of it. They even desert their precious "Fatherland" directly it is in sore straits.

I expect tomorrow we shall get the finest, most splendid news of all, that the Armistice is really & truly signed.

# The Kaiser (!!)

## The "All-Highest" (!!) The "War Lord" (!)

Dethroned; crushed; conquered; humiliated; disgraced; and loathed now and for ever more for the countless crimes he has committed; the unspeakable cruelties he has condoned; and the millions of human beings he has slain throughout Europe.

# King George.

## " GOD SAVE THE KING. "

Monday 11th Nov. 19.18. **PEACE** ! The armistice is signed, "the day" has come at last, and — it is ours! Every heart is vibrating to the wonderful song of Triumph that swells throughout the Empire this day. The War is over! and We have Won the War, & glory, honour and Victory is our

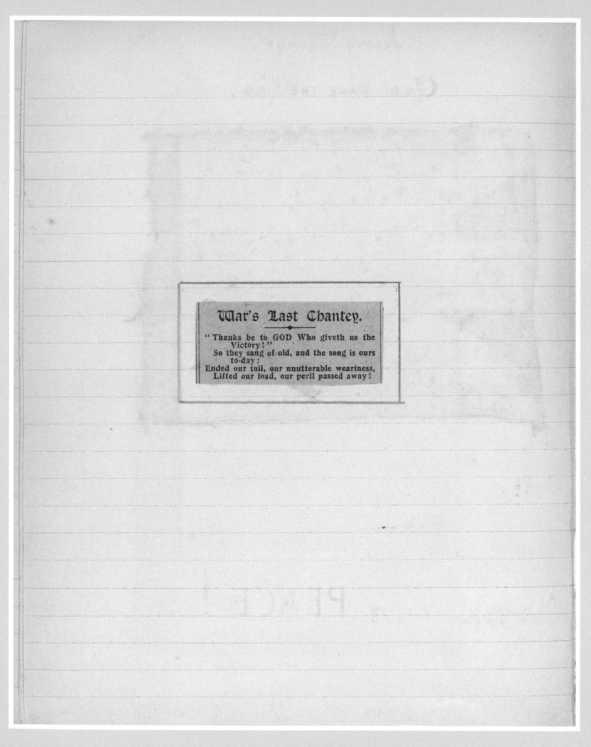

**War's Last Chantey.**

"Thanks be to GOD Who giveth us the
    Victory!"
So they sang of old, and the song is ours
    to-day:
Ended our toil, our unutterable weariness,
Lifted our load, our peril passed away!

(Monday 11th Nov. con.) More than four years ago at the outset of the War, when all England was thrilling with Excitement, I bought this small Union Jack, and stuck it up over the mantlepiece. There it stayed some weeks, getting dusty — but still preserving

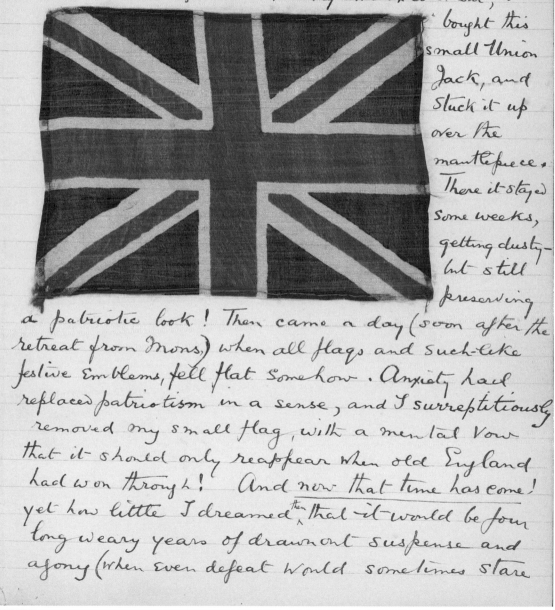

a patriotic look! Then came a day (soon after the retreat from Mons,) when all flags and such-like festive Emblems, fell flat somehow. Anxiety had replaced patriotism in a sense, and I surreptitiously removed my small flag, with a mental vow that it should only reappear when old England had won through! And now that time has come! yet how little I dreamed then that it would be four long weary years of drawn out suspense and agony (when even defeat would sometimes stare

us in the face) before right could conquer might. So I have put this small trophy in my War diary, because it is really quite a historic little flag, and could tell a tale of the Great War to succeeding generations from beginning to end, almost from that crucial moment when the Edict went forth "England has sent an ultimatum to Germany", down to the signing of the Armistice this morning !!

Today has been a truly wonderful day, and I'm glad I was alive to see it! From the moment one got out of bed, this 11th of November, there was a sort of feeling in the air that something was going to happen! And yet we all felt doubtful of Germany up to the very last, and half expected some new act of treachery at the eleventh hour. I was trying to write a coherent letter this morning (rather a difficult proceeding under the circumstances!) when all of a sudden the air was rent by a tremendous **Bang** !!. My instant thought was — a raid! for our maroons have become so interwoven with the horrors of Gothas & bombs

that it has become almost impossible to dissociate
them. But when another great explosion
shook the windows, and the hooters at Woolwich
began to scream like things demented, and the
guns started frantically firing all round
us like an almighty fugue, (!) I knew that
this was no raid, but that the signing of the
Armistice had been accomplished! Signal upon
signal took up the news; the glorious pulverising
news, — that the End had come at last, and the
greatest war in history was over.

London went quite mad and let itself
go. Pandemonium reigned everywhere; bells
burst out into chimes, guns "vollied & thundered",
sirens and hooters screamed, while people sang,
waved, cheered, shouted, rang dinner bells,
and lost their heads generally!

But I think the most impressive sight of all
must have been that in front of Buckingham Palace.
Here vast crowds assembled, all shouting out at the
tops of their voices "We want the King"! So the King
and Queen, and young Princess Mary, came out on to
the balcony to be greeted by a roar of cheers,

and when the King could be heard he said —
"With you I rejoice and thank GOD for the victories"
"which the allied armies have won, bringing"
"hostilities to an end, and peace with-in sight."
And even our usually self-contained Queen grew excited
and waved a flag! and they must all have felt pretty
chokey, (what) with their thousands of loyal subjects all
round them waving & yelling, and the bands playing
"GOD save the King" and the "Old Hundredth"! Even to read
about it all in the papers makes one feel like crying!
This historic scene terminated by the band striking up
"Old Lang Syne", and then King George, waving his hat, went
back into the Palace followed by the Queen & "little Mary"!
(And I guess they all said their prayers that night.)

REMEMBER ALWAYS
FINE ✦ ART        TRADE ✦ GUILD
NOTHING GERMAN

The Great War has lasted :—
4 Years,
14 Weeks,
2 Days.

> ## PEACE.
>
> Bow down, Old Land, at the altar-steps of
>   God—
>   Thank Him for Peace, thank Him for
>     Victory;
> But thank Him chiefly that thy feet have
>   trod
> The path of honour, in the Agony. .
>
> J. S. ARKWRIGHT.

1918.

November 11th .
Armistice Day.

# DIARY OF THE GREAT WAR.

**1914.**

July 28—Austria-Hungary declares war on Serbia.
Aug. 1—Germany declares war on Russia.
   ,, 0—Germany declares war on France.
   ,, 4—Great Britain declares war on Germany.
   ,, 12—State of war declared between Great Britain and Austria-Hungary.
   ,, 16—Expeditionary force landed in France.
   ,, 23—Japan declares war on Germany.
Sept. 5—End of retreat from Mons to Marne.
Nov. 5—Great Britain declares war on Turkey.
Dec. 8—Naval battle off Falkland.

**1915.**

April 27—Allied troops land in Gallipoli.
May 7—Lusitania torpedoed.
   ,, 13—Italy declares war on Austria.
   ,, 25—Coalition Cabinet formed.
July 9—Conquest of German South-West Africa.
Oct. 13—Nurse Cavell murdered by Germans.
   ,, 14—Bulgaria at war with Serbia.

**1916.**

Jan. 8—Complete evacuation of Gallipoli.
May 3—Compulsory Military Service Bill.
   ,, 31—Battle of Jutland.
June 5—Lord Kitchener drowned.
July 1—Somme battle began.
   ,, 27—Captain Fryatt shot by Germans.
Aug. 27—Rumania declares war on Austria-Hungary. Italy declares war on Germany.
Dec. 7—Mr. Lloyd George Prime Minister.

**1917.**

March 11—British take Bagdad.
   ,, 12—Revolution in Russia.
April 5—United States at war with Germany.
Nov. 18—General Maude, victor of Bagdad, died in Mesopotamia.
Dec. 9—Fall of Jerusalem.

**1918.**

March 3—Treaty of Brest-Litovsk concluded between Germans and Bolsheviks.
   ,, 21—Kaiser's battle to " crush " British Army opens on fifty-mile front.
April 9—Mr. Lloyd George introduced Bill raising Army age to fifty.—(Passed.)
July 16—Tsar shot by Bolsheviks.
   ,, 18—Great French counter-attack begins.
Aug. 8—Sir D. Haig attacks on twenty-mile front.
Sept. 15—Austria's offer to discuss peace.
   ,, 30—Bulgaria surrenders unconditionally.
Oct. 6—Germany, Austria and Turkey seek peace through President Wilson.
   ,, 17—British naval force landed at Ostend. Lille captured by British.
   ,, 27—Ludendorff resigns.
   ,, 28—Austria pleads for separate peace.
   ,, 31—Allied armistice with Turkey.
Nov. 4—Armistice with Austria takes effect.
   ,, 9—Kaiser abdicates. Crown Prince also signs a renunciation.
   ,, 11—Armistice signed at 5 a.m. Hostilities cease at 11 a.m.

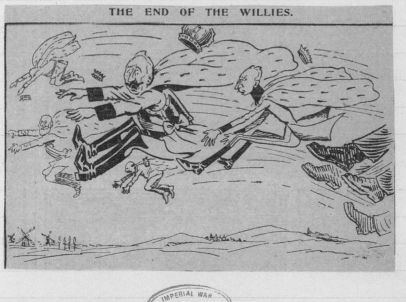

## THE END OF THE WILLIES.

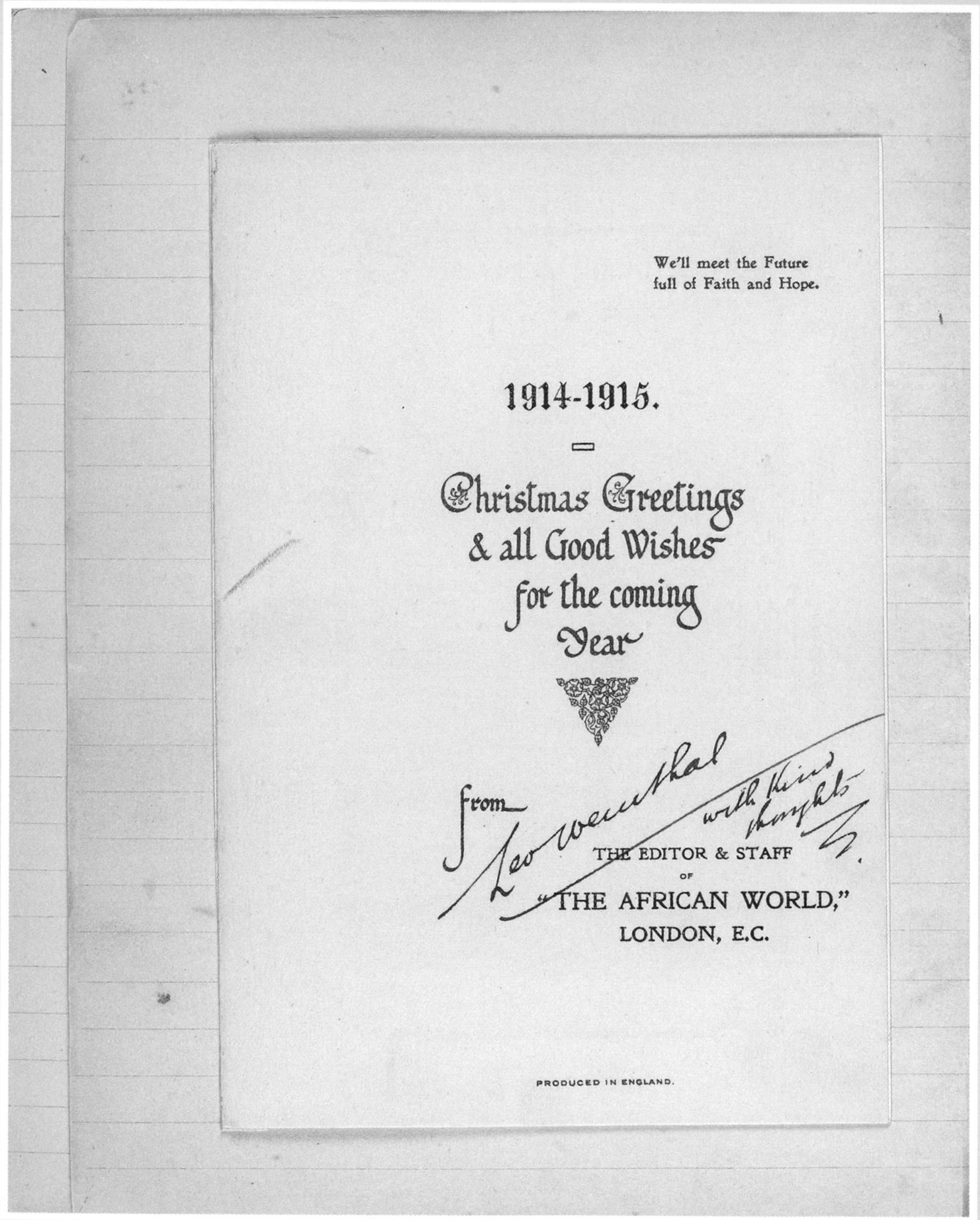

We'll meet the Future
full of Faith and Hope.

# 1914-1915.

## Christmas Greetings
## & all Good Wishes
## for the coming
## Year

from *Leo Weinthal* with kind thoughts

THE EDITOR & STAFF

OF

"THE AFRICAN WORLD,"

LONDON, E.C.

PRODUCED IN ENGLAND.

PART TWO

# Ethel M. Bilbrough, My War Diary 1914-1918

Ethel Bilbrough's title for her diary shows the flags of the Allies — Japan, France, Britain, Russia and Belgium — at the start of the war.

Horatio Herbert Kitchener, 1st Earl Kitchener (1850-1916) was Secretary of State for War, 1914-16). His call for volunteers increased the size of Britain's army by hundreds of thousands.

# July 15th, 1915

This is going to be my war diary. I don't mean that it's to be political, or literary, or anything of that kind, but it will merely be my own personal impressions, and I shan't even touch on the *fringe* of the vast problem as to what has caused the greatest war that has ever been known in history, or as to what will be likely to terminate it all!

It seems to me that everyone who happens to be alive in such stirring epoch-making times, ought to write *something* of what is going on! Just think how interesting it would be to read years hence when peace once more reigns supreme, and everything has settled down to its usual torpid routine of dullness!

Terrible as it all is, I think I'd rather be living now than, say in early Victorian days! Now everyone *is* living and no mistake about it, there's no more playing at things. "Life is real and life is earnest," and I doubt if it will ever seem quite the same again as it did before this great European war.

One wonders now what one did in days of peace! What *did* people do? What did they talk about? What did they read about? What did they think about? (If they ever thought at all!) But moral reflections are always rather boring! And I am wondering how I will start on the difficult subject before me!

I can hardly realise that it is nearly a year ago since we were all thrown into the wildest excitement at even the *prospect* of a "war with Germany"! Up to the very last I don't think anyone really believed we should fight, and I remember how staggered we were one Sunday morning last August, when walking over the common to Church, we passed a man engrossed in a Sunday paper which announced in large letters that war was proclaimed between England and Germany! *Then* somehow or other, it all seemed much nearer and much more real! Of course one had been following with deep interest the fighting with Servia and brave little Belgium, but that *we* should be drawn in, was quite another matter!

But one little realised then what it was all to mean in the future to *us*, the appalling loss of life, the sacrifice, the horror of it all! Yet it is now raging – no abatement of the cruel slaughter, it just goes on from day to day increasing in venom and hatred, and loss of life. Oh! That such a thing as war should be *possible* in these enlightened civilised (?) days!

JULY 15TH 1915

It has evolved so gradually! Last August the state of things (as they exist now) would have been thought unspeakable! But step by step it has grown to what it now is, though in early days before the real fighting had begun, one never dreamed of such possibilities.

We went to the wilds of North Wales in September last, and expected to get right out of the war zone and all its news, and I shall never forget what an uncomfortable start it gave me when, turning a sharp corner on the isolated slopes of Snowdon one day, we were suddenly faced by a soldier in khaki with fixed bayonet, who calmly challenged us! One felt indignant at first, then amused, and finally we replied with surprising humility, that we were "merely taking a walk"!

I wish I had started this book when the war actually first began! But it never entered my head then! One imagined the whole thing would be all over and forgotten in a few months. It is a great mercy that the things which are to come are veiled from us.

So I must try and go back in memory to the first early months of fighting last Autumn, when it was all fresh and thrilling, with an undercurrent of excitement and romance.

One of the first things that struck me was the dreadful

## MEN AND WOMEN OF ENGLAND.

A ruthless and relentless foe seeks to grind under its heel your Country and your Liberty.

You are called upon to light your lamps of sacrifice.

To send every fit man to the Front—your Sons, your Brothers, your Friends, and to pray to God that they may return unharmed.

Your succour is wanted for those who are left behind—in money. in help, in sympathy.

We people of England will rise to the height of our strength and of our patriotism.

We will shew by the sacrifice we are prepared to make the value we place on the freedom of our Country and the sacredness of our homes.

By the help of God we will hand down these blessings unimpaired to our children.

We are out to Fight and to Conquer.

### For God—For King—For Country.

SEPTEMBER, 1914.

Patriotic poster of September 1914, rallying the population and calling for support for the war effort.

cruelty to the poor dear innocent horses! Men fight *voluntarily*, but the horses are dragged into the sickening melee to suffer and go through untold agonies all through no fault of their own, it seems so unfair to them.

## TOUCHING MEMORIAL

By the pulpit is a small bronze model of a good, fat Army horse. And underneath is written:—

"In grateful and reverent memory of the Empire's horses (some 375,000) who fell in the Great War. Most obediently and often most painfully they died—'*Faithful unto Death, not one of them is Forgotten before God.*'"

Beautiful!

Annotated 'Ten years afterwards! [1928]' by the author, this cutting shows that the horses of the Great War were remembered.

## AN APPEAL.

I'm only a cavalry charger,
  And I'm dying as fast as I can
(For my body is riddled with bullets—
  They've potted both me and my man);
And though I've no words to express it,
  I'm trying this message to tell
To kind folks who work for the Red Cross—
  Oh, please help the Blue one as well!

My master was one in a thousand,
  And I loved him with all my poor heart
(For horses are built just like humans,
  Be kind to them—they'll do their part);
So please send out help for our wounded,
  And give us a word in your prayers;
This isn't so strange as you'd fancy—
  The Russians do it in theirs.

I'm only a cavalry charger,
  And my eyes are becoming quite dim
(I really don't mind though I'm "done for,"
  So long as I'm going to *him*);
But first I would plead for my comrades,
  Who're dying and suffering, too—
Oh, please help the poor wounded horses!
  I'm sure that you would—if you knew.

SCOTS GREYS.

This anonymous poem appeals for support for the work of the Blue Cross and other animal charities.

**JULY 15TH 1915**

## FOR THE HORSES.

I CHANCED to be at Waterloo Station when several fine horses were patiently waiting to be taken off to the war, and the thought struck me how infinitely sad it is to contemplate the terrible pain that these poor creatures may be called upon to bear when left to die slowly, and in torment, on the battlefield.

Can no one suggest a means whereby these suffering animals could be mercifully put out of their misery at the end of an encounter?

Of course, the men come first, for whom our hearts are aching with sympathy, but have we none to spare for the friend of man, the noble cavalry horse, who has to suffer u n t o l d agony caused by shrapnel and other hideous inventions of the civilised world?

What practical effort can be made besides the expression of our sympathy in words? Perhaps some readers of *The Daily Mirror* will think out a remedy that might help in this good cause.       E. M. B.

Chislehurst.

Ethel Bilbrough's letter of 2nd August 1914 to the *Daily Mirror* was published a week after the war started: one of the earliest expressions of concern about the welfare of horses in war.

Examples of two of the flags sold to raise money to help injured animals.

Of course it is a most fearfully difficult question, as modern warfare is so totally different to what it was. *Now* the range of a battlefield will extend for miles and miles, and who can be found to traverse it in order to give relief to the dying horse when there are men lying all along the line wounded and suffering? Yet if only something could be done to end the sufferings of our poor war horses who are terribly hurt, by a quick merciful death! The dreadful, *hideous* cruelty lies in letting them die by inches . . . it is too horrible to contemplate. I wrote the following letter to the Mirror and it was printed. [See text page 148, bottom left.]

Of course such letters may not do one particle of good, but at least they can do no harm, and someone *may* read them who can help try and solve the difficulty.

And so when I feel very strongly about a thing, it is always a relief to put pen to paper!

There were answers to this, and several societies have lately done what they can, especially the Blue Cross Society, and the Veterinary Corps, etc. But my consolation is that my letter came at the very commencement of the war for I wrote it on August 11th, 1914.

How little we dreamed last July in 1914 of all that was impending! We had actually decided to go to Rothenburg for our Autumn holiday! And indeed it was a *very* near thing, for if the war had come a few weeks later, or we had started a few weeks earlier, we should most certainly have all been taken prisoners! How little I thought of the deadly enmity and hatred that would come so soon between ourselves and Germany as I racked my brains for a couple of hours every morning over the horrible German language in order to be able to hold forth, and give orders on the Rothenburg trip! It is a mercy the future is always a sealed book. Still, things looked ominous even from the first, and the following entry occurs in my day diary on July 28th 1914. "Getting all the information we can about Rothenburg, but I doubt if we shall be able to go there after all, as owing to this fighting between Austria and Servia there is just

The Stronger.—F. Matania.

Fortunino Matania
(1881-1963) was
an Italian painter
working in London
who became a war
artist. His emotive
and realistic work was
much admired.

the hideous possibility of an European War"! How soon it became a hideous fact!

Then poor brave little Belgium was drawn in, and Germany began to show her poisonous fangs, and the poor Belgians were driven right and left, homeless and destitute, and their homes pillaged and burnt. But I do love this picture! For the small Belgian is scoring off the hateful German officer for once — who, for the moment, is helpless!

No sooner was England's ultimatum to Germany given out, than stirring events came tumbling over each other's heels with amazing rapidity. France was drawn in soon after Russia, and so the dreaded European war commenced in grim earnest. Germany and Austria against the allies of England, France, Servia, Russia, Belgium — and later on, Italy. They had chosen a hard nut to crack, those Germans! But they have been preparing for war (especially against England) for years and years, only we never would realise or believe it! We are always *late* in waking up to facts, and we have still much to learn as a nation.

Poor Belgium soon came to grief, though her men fought valiantly and made a noble stand against the enemy, but they were not strong enough, and one after another — Namur, Luxembourg, Liege, and Brussels all had to be evacuated, and taken possession of by the Germans, who ceased to behave as men, and became devils. This is what war does to civilisation.

England rapidly began to change too under war conditions, yet so naturally does one thing merge into another, that one hardly comprehends all that is actually going on around us. Although such stupendous things are taking place, there are still thousands of people to whom the war has made but little material difference in their mode of life — although of course to others it has brought suffering and sorrow and loss.

> **A Year of War.** July 1915.
>
> This time last year we were on the brink of War. And such a War! It has cost the nation already many thousands of brave lives, the suffering of scores of thousands of wounded men, the desolation of many homes, and five hundred millions of pounds! But, who if told a year ago that the nation in the succeeding twelve months would suffer such things, would have expected us personally at home to have our wealth, health, and comfort interfered with so little?

The Rev. Canon Samuel Edward Bayard Serle was vicar of the Church of the Annunciation, Chislehurst, 1912-37. His thoughts would have been echoed in many other parish magazines across the land.

So writes Mr Serle our vicar, in his Parish Magazine for July 1915.

One cannot be thankful enough that one has no relatives fighting at the front. How *awful* that would be! How one would cry out against the injustice of fighting, I would cry out against even patriotism itself. Patriotism is a very fine thing in the abstract, but is it — *can* it ever be stronger than love? If so, then love is not "the greatest thing in the world" . . . (and it *is*).

The Huns continue their cowardly dastardly attacks on poor brave little Belgium. They have not the slightest regard for the lives of women and children and even the churches are treated in the same way. They care for neither God nor the devil — though indeed it often looks as if Germany (and especially the Kaiser!) were in league with the latter! Here is a specimen of the havoc they delight in making of a church — this shows the altar.

JULY 15TH
1915

A priest standing among the ruins of his once beautiful church in Termonde after its destruction by the Germans.

The damage to the church in Termonde was typical of damage to ecclesiastical and civilian property across the whole area of the Western Front.

On the 17th Dec. 1914, the Germans sent over a fleet of cruisers and bombarded our east coast towns of Scarborough, Whitby and Hartlepool, killing many civilians and several women, children and babies — which is apparently their idea of valour and chivalry! Over 100 lives were lost — or rather were massacred.

I suppose the last time England's shores were attacked by an enemy must have been when the Danes indulged in their raids! But it is horrible to think that such things can take place in these enlightened (?) days, but then the Germans are proving every day that they have no sense of right or justice, or morality or honour.

*Right and below:* House in Scarborough where three dead bodies were found after the bombardment.

## GERMAN BOMBARDMENT.

A house in the Crescent, Scarborough, which was shattered by a German shell fired from a Dreadnought cruiser.

There is khaki everywhere now, one is getting quite used to it. *England at war!* It sounds like some half forgotten fairy story of schoolroom days — when one sat through the long morning hours toiling drearily though the Wars of the Roses in "Little Arthur's History of England"! Khaki Bibles and khaki prayer books even, are now bound up and sold for our soldiers, and Lord Roberts — dear good man that he was — wrote the words that I have put in above [see below], and now they are bound up in every little khaki prayer book, on the first page. If only England had listened to Lord Roberts' words of warning to us after the Boer War, we should be better equipped for the present desperate encounter.

## BIBLES FOR THE TROOPS.

### MESSAGE IN EACH FROM LORD ROBERTS.

Lord Roberts, through the medium of the Scripture Gifts Mission and the Naval and Military Bible Society, has addressed the following words to the troops on home and foreign service:—

I ask you to put your trust in God. He will watch over you and strengthen you. You will find in this little book guidance when you are in health, comfort when you are in sickness, and strength when you are in adversity.

ROBERTS, F.M.

Lord Roberts' message to the troops.

LORD ROBERTS

Frederick Sleigh Roberts, Earl Roberts (1832-1914), had fought with success in Afghanistan, India and South Africa. Commander-in-Chief of the British Army 1901-04, he was held in very high esteem.

# Christmas 1914

There was no talk of "A Merry Christmas" *this* year. No one wanted to be merry even. With all the horrors of war, no one could feel "Christmassy".

It sounded so strange the first time we had "God Save the King" sung in church *as a prayer* — the congregation all kneeling with bowed heads and singing it seriously, slowly, and reverently.

It usually comes as a finish to mirthful festivities, or as a wind-up to some rollicking entertainment, but now that is all changed, and so has the significance of the fine old national anthem.

The next step that seemed queer and unusual, (and rather awesome at first!) were the things we began to offer up prayers for in church every Sunday. For war hospitals, the "sick and wounded", for "nurses", "doctors", "army chaplains", for those who serve their country on sea and land, "*or in the air*"!

Then later on, lists of names were read out for those to be prayed for, and the list of sick and wounded and for dying and dead, grew so terribly long that at last it had to be divided up at the different services.

Barry Eric Odell Pain (1864-1928) was an English journalist, poet and author. His work appeared in publications such as the *Cornhill Magazine*, *Punch*, and the *Daily Chronicle*.

## THE KAISER AND GOD.

### BY BARRY PAIN.

"I rejoice with you in Wilhelm's first victory. How magnificently God supported him!"

Led by Wilhelm, as you tell,
God has done extremely well;
You with patronizing nod
Show that you approve of God.
Kaiser, face a question new—
This—does God approve of you?

Broken pledges, treaties torn
Your first page of war adorn;
We on fouler things must look
Who read further in that book,
Where you did in time of war
All that you in peace forswore,
Where you, barbarously wise,
Bade your soldiers terrorize,
Where you made—the deed was fine—
Women screen your firing line,
Villages burned down to dust,
Torture, murder, bestial lust,
Filth too foul for printer's ink,
Crimes from which the apes would shrink—
Strange the offerings that you press
On the God of Righteousness!

Kaiser, when you'd decorate
Sons or friends who serve your State,
Not that Iron Cross bestow
But a Cross of Wood, and so—
So remind the world that you
Have made Calvary anew,

Kaiser, when you'd kneel in prayer
Look upon your hands, and there
Let that deep and awful stain
From the blood of children slain
Burn your very soul with shame,
Till you dare not breathe that Name
That now you glibly advertise—
God as one of your allies.

Impious braggart, you forget;
God is not your conscript yet;
You shall learn in dumb amaze
That His ways are not your ways,
That the mire through which you trod
Is not the high white road of God,

*To Whom, whichever way the combat rolls,
We, fighting to the end, commend our souls.*

As I have said, there were no Christmas festivities, and only a few people sent Christmas cards. I did an original one (symbolical) of four ships coming into port, representing the allies, with their flags "en evidence"! Here it is (but somebody said the flags looked like "tin flags" so I scratched them out!)

May the New Year's rising sun

Be a Herald of Peace. (but it wasn't!)

1914 - 15.

E.M.B.

Christmas Greetings

from . . . . . . . . . . .

Ethel Bilbrough's Christmas card includes a hope for peace – but her penciled comment shows a much more pragmatic view.

The New Year 1915 started gloomily enough. The war came very near indeed when three hospitals for the wounded were opened in our own peaceful suburb of Chislehurst. In a very short time they were full, and at first we had all Belgians. Here French came in useful, and I felt very thankful I could talk it, for none of the men could speak one word of English of course. I drove some of them out, and it was quite entertaining, they were such nice refined men, not a bit vulgar or common.

On the 1st of January I got up a concert for them at Holbrook, and we had mostly French songs, though several of the men had picked up the tune and words of "Tipperary", and sang in the chorus lustily with their funny broken English.

Then came the Belgian refugees, and again Chislehurst opened her ever hospitable arms, and received several of these poor outcasts at two beautiful houses on the Common, prepared and furnished entirely for them, even down to pianos! Many people took three or four refugees into their own homes for months at a time, a most Christian thing to do! Because it is a terrible thing to part with the peace and privacy of one's own four walls (whatever is happening outside them!) Chislehurst has certainly nothing to reproach itself with, for *how* these Belgians and the Belgian patients in the hospitals were cared for and looked after! And concerts were got up for them constantly, and teas, and entertainments, and they were driven out in motors and carriages, and feted, and amused, and spoilt to such an extent, it's a wonder they were not all quite ruined! It proved later on not to be particularly good for them! And the teas were stopped, and the concerts more limited, and none of the men allowed to go out unless attended by someone in authority. Of course the men hated this, and they felt it fearfully undignified having to go for walks with a lady to see they didn't "get into mischief"! But then they brought it on themselves and deserved it, since when they *had* their liberty they came home to the hospital on more than one occasion, extremely tipsy! So the only

— 157 —

## WALKS FOR THE WOUNDED.

IN THE suburb where I live there are a considerable number of wounded soldiers. A stringent rule has been passed at the hospitals which forbids any of the patients being allowed out unless attended by some responsible person, and, owing to the scarcity of men just at present, this task naturally falls to any local lady who is willing to take the soldiers for walks.

But, strange though it may appear, there exists a considerable amount of prejudice on this point, and I have heard it asserted more than once that such a course of proceeding is neither dignified nor desirable, and that all wounded soldiers ought to be escorted out by men only.

Now it happens that every man who is not actually fighting is just as fully occupied as he can be, so things have to be faced as they are and not as they might be.

Surely it is the height of selfishness for any woman not engaged in definite work for the war to shirk this obvious duty lest she offend conventionality. Can she sit comfortably at home with a clear conscience, knowing all the while that several wounded and weary Tommies are being kept cooped up in a limited space, though longing to stretch their tired limbs and get a glimpse of new surroundings, just because she hesitates to take these poor fellows out into the sunshine and give them a good airing?

Of course, a young girl might not prove a suitable escort for many reasons, one being that it is by no means an easy undertaking, since it is often very tiring both physically and mentally. One cannot walk along in silence, and it requires considerable tact to steer the conversation into fitting channels without its becoming either dull or familiar!

But one thing I am certain of, and that is, the men appreciate the effort, and the companionship of a lady always has a refining influence even on the roughest character, and this in itself is a good thing apart from any question of exercise and fresh air.        E. M. B.

Ethel Bilbrough's letter to the *Mirror* argues for common sense, as well as patriotism.

thing to be done was not to allow them to go out at all without an escort.

Chislehurst is an exceedingly 'proper' and correct suburb — though I suppose all small towns are alike in this respect! And there were those who disapproved of the men being taken out by the opposite sex, which seemed very narrow and bigoted! And feeling rather strongly I wrote this letter to the Mirror which appears on this page.

Certainly I preferred the Belgians to the English Tommies, because they are inately refined and respectful. They never forgot at the end of a walk or a drive to salute, and say gratefully "Merci bien, Madame", but the English fellows would just slope off after a walk with never a "thank you", or even a "good morning"! But of course no one takes the poor wounded lads out for "thanks", and one has to remember that probably a heart of real English gold beats under the undemonstrative English khaki coat!

On the 7th May (1915) all Europe was thrown into a state of consternation at a diabolical act of the German fiends! They actually torpedoed (and sank) one of our largest liners, the "Lusitania" coming from America; and twelve hundred civilians — American, English, and many other harmless and helpless people were ruthlessly drowned without a chance of escape.

Words entirely fail to express what all England — and America too — felt at this unparalleled outrage. America talked a lot, and threatened Germany if such a thing "ever occurred again", but it all ended in smoke, and was soon forgotten — except by the poor sorrowing relatives of the 1,200 souls whose bodies lay at the bottom of the sea, all because Germany is at war. The relentless wickedness of such an act has not its like in all history I should think.

But the Germans become more inhuman every day.

One of the strangest things in life is, how soon one becomes used to a new and altered state of circumstances! For instance, on going up to London now, say on a Saturday to dine and go to a theatre, everything is quite different to what it was before the war. There are fewer trains, and the ones which do continue to run are horribly crowded. The passengers are mostly in khaki. Young subalterns, and officers, and colonels, all passing on their way to the front, with no idea as to whether they will ever return to the old country again, or rest (for all time) in foreign lands.

At the restaurants too, every table has its boy or full-fledged man in the khaki uniform which has become so common. Some of the tables are occupied by wounded soldiers, and the last time we were at the "Coventry" having dinner, there was next to us, a young fellow calmly enjoying himself with the whole of his head bound up in a white bandage! Yet no one even glanced at him, though a year ago he would probably have been politely asked by the manager to vacate his seat!

Then returning after dark, everything is changed. London is thrown into complete obscurity on account of a possible Zeppelin raid! Instead of the brilliantly lit up streets, the rows of coloured lights at the various music halls and cinemas, the electric lights everywhere, their reflection flickering in the river along the Embankment, *now* all is plunged in comparative darkness. Only a light where it is absolutely necessary, and it is positively dangerous to cross the roads. Directly dusk appears, all the blinds have to be pulled down in the trains for fear of *hostile aircraft*, and one reads this in every railway carriage.

MAY
1915

**SOUTH EASTERN AND CHATHAM RAILWAY.**

# IMPORTANT NOTICE.

**Passengers are requested to see that the Blinds in this Compartment are pulled down after dark, except while the Train is standing at the Station.**

**This is necessary in order to conform to the requirements of the Government.**

Much continues to be talked and written about on the subject of *economy* in war time. It is very necessary, for the price of everything continues to go up so alarmingly, and taxation is becoming heavier and heavier in order to meet the appalling demands the war makes upon us. The government is now spending *three million a day*: it is difficult to take in all that such a sum means.

But extravagance is at all times a silly and ostentatious thing. We should be much happier if we all lived simpler lives whether with a view to saving for the country or otherwise, and it's really rather a good thing that people are now forced "to pull up" whether they like it or not! England had been getting fearfully luxurious and self-indulgent and, it is to be feared, rather slack and effeminate too, and nothing short of an awful war like this would have brought her as a nation to her senses and her knees.

William Kerridge
Haselden (1872-
1953) was known
for the gentle social
commentary of his
cartoons.

**MAY**
**1915**

When the war ends, I wonder if people will keep on with their
new cautious way of living? Or whether they will return recklessly
to former extravagances and with renewed zeal for having been

Comments on economy, by Arthur Bilbrough (1840-1925). He was Ethel's father-in-law, and had built up a considerable business in shipping and marine insurance, which by this date was run by Ethel's husband Kenneth. Arthur Bilbrough lived near them in Chislehurst.

obliged to discontinue it for so long a time! But certainly people are happier when they cease to be epicures and gourmands, as Haselden cleverly shows on the following skit. [See cartoon on p161.]

It will be a thousand pities if we drift back into the old spendthrift ways directly peace is proclaimed, though in truth that day seems a long way off, for we are still in a very dark tunnel, where, however much we may strain our eyes, no sign of the end can be seen.

People love to speculate on how long this war will last! Some say "6 months", others "another year", but I believe it will be a good while longer. Germany will hold on like a bulldog to her last gasp, and the English and French will *never* give in — at least one hopes not! — so there we are! And there we shall remain apparently, as long as there are *any men left alive to fight*!

It's a pity women don't fight (I mean more than they do!)

Ethel Bilbrough's letter makes practical and sensible suggestions for entertaining economically.

# Wednesday 30th June, 1915

Today was the day set apart to collect funds for our Allies, the French. Flags were sold in every street and huge sums of money were collected. Where all the money comes from is a marvel! The calls upon it are colossal yet it never seems to run dry, and the Prince of Wales' Fund for those who suffer "by reason of the war", has now reached a total of over five million pounds. Certainly this war, awful as it is, is bringing out all the generosity and Christian charity there is in the world, with a vengeance!

There is a great deal talked about the "entente cordiale" just now between us and the French — I wonder if its cordiality is of an *abiding* nature? These little medals were also sold today for the French Red Cross Fund, and most of the men wore one on their coats.

*Top:* Joseph Jacques Césaire Joffre (1852-1931) became French commander-in-chief in 1916, although he had never commanded an army. He was chiefly responsible for the victory on the Marne in September 1914 which stopped the German advance on Paris.

*Left:* Ethel Bilbrough describes this as the 'French Relief Fund Medal', a popular fund-raiser.

## JUNE 30TH 1915

William Harry Toy (1885-1915) was a self-taught artist who worked as political cartoonist for the *Daily Sketch*. He also worked for *Punch* and the *Daily Mirror*. In 1915 there weren't enough munitions workers, and those there were had to work long hours. Some went on strike, asking for an extra ha'penny, so they could meet rising prices. Many thought the strike displayed a lack of patriotism.

By hindering the output of munitions of war the workmen on strike are playing the part of the Kaiser's friend.

# August 1915

A warm weary month, when people's hearts were sinking at the prospect of another winter's war. For surely this terrible fighting will continue; there is no sign of a rift in the clouds, and the pessimist looks glum, and the optimist is silent. War, war, war, and our brave lads are being hacked and shot down day by day in appalling numbers. One wonders if there will be any men left at all in the world at the present rate of extermination; it will be a world of women before long — *what an awful place!*

There was much talk this month as to whether it was justifiable to take a holiday or not as usual, and I think everyone agreed that it was *more* necessary than ever this year, when men's hearts are failing them. Things do not look bright, and no one can foresee the end of it all.

They say that the Kaiser — that slayer of millions — has aged 20 years since this war began, and he now looks worn and haggard and weary; and well he may!

> Our losses are heavy. They were bound to be. We shall bear them stoically, as is our duty, not inquiring whether any could have been avoided until the time comes for such inquiry, but remembering that, heavy as is the toll of life, it is less than that of our Allies, and far less than that of the enemy. Therein lies our hope for the future. We have lost in killed in round numbers seventy thousand men; the most trustworthy estimates of the German losses indicate that their total of killed reaches well over a million, and their rate of loss, which has been heavier than that of all the Allies throughout, continues disproportionately heavy.

This cutting shows how newspapers tried to keep up morale while admitting that losses had occurred.

# Thursday 7th October, 1915

Two months since I wrote in this book! And yet everything is going on in the same dreary drawn out manner, and the death toll of our brave manly English boys is increasing horribly day by day. We have been away for our autumn holiday, but the war dogged our footsteps, and once while placidly sketching on the cliff, a khaki sentinel approached me and calmly demanded my sketchbook, as sketching was forbidden within three miles of the coast! I had to give it up of course, but relieved myself by saying some *most* unchristian things!

Army Form O. 348.

**MEMORANDUM.**

From O. C. Cyclist Detachment,
Portland Garrison.
The Nothe,
Weymouth

To Miss E. M. Bilbrough
Chiselhurst
Kent

29th July 1915.

Herewith please find the sketch book taken from you at Lulworth Cove.

But after a few weeks I got my sketchbook back safe and sound, with the accompanying notice! And it amused one to think what a lot of trouble these good people had given themselves over a practically empty, and harmless little sixpenny sketchbook! However, it has given me another memento of the war to stick in here!

An interesting example of how military need impinged on civilian life.

# Thursday 7th October (*continued*)
## Italian Flag Day

Ribbon and flag sold to raise money for Italy, which had joined the Allies in 1915.

Today was the Italian Flag Day, and London was full of the little penny flags of Italy's colours. One little flag just like the one I give here below [see right] was sold for fifty pounds! But of course all the money went to help Italy and her soldiers as they are now our Allies, though comparatively recent ones. I think the English nation is a most remarkably generous one. Only the other day they were "shelling" out for the French red cross day, and now the Englishman's hand is once more in his pocket for Italy! It is wonderful, simply wonderful where all the money comes from! People have only to ask and they get, fortunately.

**OCTOBER 7TH 1915**

Now that Italy has thrown in her part with our Allies, and that Bulgaria has thrown in *her* lot against us with Turkey, nearly all Europe is now fighting in this ghastly war, as will be easily seen by the printed list here.

A useful summary of nations involved in the war – and an interesting list of neutral states.

## NATIONS AT WAR.

### NEARLY THE WHOLE OF EUROPE ENGAGED.

With the declaration of war by Italy on Bulgaria, the only nations in Europe not now engaged in the present gigantic struggle are Spain, Rumania, Holland, Switzerland, Greece, Denmark, Sweden, and Norway.

It was on July 28 last year that Austria threw down the gauntlet, and opened hostilities with Serbia. Thereafter events developed in the following dramatic fashion:—

1914.
Aug. 1.—Germany declares war on Russia.
" 3.—Germany " " " France.
" 4.—Britain " " " Germany.
" 10.—France " " " Austria.
" 12.—Britain " " " Austria.
" 23.—Japan " " " Germany.
Nov. 5.—Britain " " " Turkey.
1915.
May 23.—Italy " " " Austria.
Aug. 20.—Italy " " " Turkey.
Oct. 15.—Britain " " " Bulgaria.
" 16.—France " " " Bulgaria.
" 19.—Italy " " " Bulgaria.

Serbia was attacked by Bulgaria without any declaration of war. The other members of the Entente—Belgium and Montenegro—are also at war with our enemies, while the little Republic of San Marino declared herself on Italy's side. Portugal has also declared war on Germany.

# Wednesday 13th October, 1915
## (We experience our *first raid!*)

Being the night of our harvest festival, A. and I went to church as, war or no war, there's no reason why people shouldn't be grateful for a splendid harvest.

It was a lovely night — not a cloud to be seen; a fine night for Zeppelins, and an ideal one for a raid! So it proved; for on coming out of church after a nice peaceful service about "ploughing fields and harvest homes", we found Chislehurst in a most unusual state of commotion! Excited groups hung about the church porch, and we caught fragmentary bits of conversation about "bombs", and "shells" and "guns"!

In spite of the myriads of stars, it was very dark, there being no moon — goodness knows where it had got to (scared away I should think by the atrocities of mankind!) Coming home one found it expedient to walk in the middle of the road, which seemed the only place where one couldn't break one's ankle over the unseen curb, or barge into a gate or lamp post! None of which are lit now owing to the new lighting regulations. Coming along Willow Grove we met a man (in a state of abject terror) who stopped us and asked if we had "seen the Zeppelins"? He was an extremely poor and common man, but excitement and danger makes everyone equal.

Things seemed to quiet down after that, and as we walked down Walden Road and came out at the opening at the end, there was nothing to be seen but a great arc of indigo blue sky scintillating with countless stars. A few stragglers hung about the lodges as if half hoping to hear another gun! But it was all as silent as the grave, and we slipped quietly into the Grange as the servants were all abed (that sounds nice and old fashioned!) and retired for the night. But somehow I couldn't sleep to save my life, everything was quiet, but I heard imaginary noises and held my breath listening. So an hour or two passed, and then quite audibly and *quite* unmistakably a cannon went off, bang–bang, bang bang *bang*! And (extremely alarmed) I woke up Ken sleeping the sleep of the just! A Zeppelin raid either makes a person intensely valiant, or a pitiful coward!

Ken was annoyed at being disturbed, and muttering something about "Gott strafen the Kaiser", turned over and went to sleep again! But the great guns at Woolwich (only six miles away) went on thundering away, and I wondered what was going on, and whether destruction and suffering and loss of life were really and truly taking place so near at hand. Things in the paper always seem so far away, it's only when one sees and hears *for oneself*, that the real horror of war becomes apparent. Then presently, amid the booming of guns, came a terrific sort of explosion, like a crash of several cannon going off altogether, and whatever it was, I knew it was something deathly — probably a bomb, and out of bed I hopped and lit a candle. The air seemed alive with horrid, weird, uncanny sounds, and there is something terrifying in the thought that two miles up above one in space there is a merciless enemy dropping incendiary bombs promiscuously on whatever comes handy!

Ken actually *did* get up then (of his own free will!) and got into a dressing gown, and we went into the oriel room in the dark.

There the window was all alight with the reflection of search lights, and shells from our guns being hurled up into the sky trying to reach the Zeppelin, and then as we got to the windows, a shell burst just like a firework, with a lurid red light. But we never reach the Zeppelins, which (*two miles* high) merely look down on our breaking shells fathoms below, and laugh! It was horribly cold standing there shivering in the dark room and watching weird things going on in the heavens, and Ken soon observed that he was "going back to bed". As there seemed nothing else to be done I followed suit, but sleep didn't come for the rest of the night, and I was very thankful to see the early dawn steal through the curtains and know that the nightmare of a night was ended. But the Zeppelins wrought havoc, and *forty two* people failed to escape, eight were killed, and the others

One of the bombs, which was apparently of a large size, penetrated the street into the subways containing the gas and water mains and in exploding melted the gas pipes, setting alight a fire which, though slight in extent, lasted for several hours.

The explosion of this bomb damaged the buildings round about considerably and destroyed almost all the glass in the neighbourhood. It was also responsible for a number of casualties, which will all be the subject of inquest. Those who were killed were either sitting in the front rooms of buildings or working or walking in the street.

The second area contains a large block of residential flats, some of which are occupied as offices. Like many other blocks of flats in London, this ٨ℛ has a stretch of garden behind the buildings, and one of the enemy's high explosive bombs fell in this garden close to the flats themselves.

Damage done to flats. Bomb burst below window.

The author labels this collection as 'Air raid over London, 13th October 1915'. The indiscriminate destruction is clear.

seriously hurt. Bombs were dropped on Woolwich where much damage was done (that was the strange, uncanny sound I heard) and about 40 fell on Croydon, while London was fiercely attacked. One side of the Strand was completely wrecked, and Ken said he went and saw where one bomb had fallen in the street, and there was a hole in the solid concrete, four feet deep! It had gone through like a red hot needle in a piece of butter! No wonder people are afraid of such demoniacal inventions; they would go slick through a house and anything (or anyone) that came in their way! All the trains were held up so that their light should be no guide, and the 8 o'clock train from town never got to Elmstead till 1 o'clock! I heard it come in, but little thought what train it was! It (the train) made an impression on me, for after the strain and anxiety of listening to unknown and terrifying sounds — sounds *never* heard before — the puffing and snorting of a railway train sounded friendly and sympathetic, and gave one a feeling of security and relief!

Next day the papers made light of it all, saying only 8 were killed and 30 wounded, but that was only up to 11.30. I *felt* there would be fresh revelations after 12 o'clock. Later on it was announced there were no fewer than 170 casualties, and over 40 deaths which is awful; five were children. Many parts of London were wrecked, including part of the Lyceum Theatre where people

## AIR RAIDS TO DATE.

| Following is a record of the Zeppelin raids this year.—*1915*. | Kld. | Injd. |
|---|---|---|
| January 19.—Yarmouth and district | 4 | 9 |
| February 21.—Colchester and Braintree | — | — |
| April 14.—Tyneside | — | 2 |
| April 16.—Lowestoft and Maldon | — | — |
| April 29.—Ipswich and Bury St. Edmunds | — | — |
| May 10.—Southend district | 1 | — |
| May 17.—Ramsgate | 2 | 8 |
| May 27.—Southend | 3 | — |
| May 31.—Outlying London | 6 | — |
| June 4.—E. and S. East Coasts | — | — |
| June 6.—East Coast | 24 | 40 |
| June 15.—North-East Coast | 16 | 14 |
| August 9.—East Coast | 15 | 14 |
| August 12.—East Coast | 6 | 23 |
| August 17.—Eastern Counties | 10 | 36 |
| September 7.—Eastern Counties | 17 | 39 |
| September 8.—Eastern Counties and London district | 38 | 124 |
| September 11.—East Coast | — | — |
| September 12.—East Coast | — | — |
| September 13.—East Coast | — | — |
| October 13.—London area | 8 | 34 |
| | *41* | *107* |

The author points out that this table shows only the damage done in the 'first year of the war (and Zeppelin raids only, not the deadly subsequent Gothas)'.

were killed, and part of the Strand is in a state of complete ruin. Bombs were simply rained down on Croydon where eight people were killed in one house, and at Woolwich (near here) great damage was done, and bombs went clean through two churches there. So that was what we heard! Not merely the firing of our cannon *at the* Zeppelins, but their own dastardly murderous bombs falling and exploding on our innocent civilians within a few miles of us.

Of course there comes up now the grave question as to whether *we* should adopt their villainous methods and drop bombs on their innocent women and children. At first it is a revolting thought and entirely repugnant to an Englishman's idea of warfare. Yet something *must* be done to put a stop to this diabolical murder, and if we retaliated it might bring these raids to an end. The German hatred to us is colossal! And the picture below depicts it cleverly.

**OCTOBER 13TH
1915**

Frank Reynolds (1876-1953) was an artist who was particularly famous for his anti-Kaiser cartoons in *Punch*. This is one of the best-known.

STUDY OF A PRUSSIAN HOUSEHOLD HAVING ITS MORNING HATE.

# Wednesday 20th October 1915

Tragedies follow each other in quick succession nowadays. Just now all England is boiling with wrath at the cold blooded murder of one of our British nurses in Belgium. Edith Cavell her name was, and she had been sheltering and befriending English and French soldiers in Belgium and helping them rejoin their regiments. Of course she knew she was defying German law! A very risky thing to attempt! She was imprisoned, tried, and almost before anyone knew anything about it, she was calmly shot in the night, or rather at 2 o'clock in the morning. What a ghastly time to be executed!

She was very brave and heroic, and declared she was "happy to die for her country", but poor soul! Her courage failed her at the

Three lines of conduct, and three only, are before us to-day: to fight, to assist the fighters, and to tend those who have fallen in the fight.

Nurse Edith Cavell, assassinated by the Germans in defiance of every law, divine and human. The Kaiser could have prevented the crime, but chose to permit it, and is chiefly responsible.

Edith Cavell, (1865-1915) the daughter of a Norfolk clergyman, trained at the London Hospital. She went to Belgium as matron of a teaching hospital, then ran a nursing journal, and supervised nursing in three hospitals as well as in schools and kindergartens.

thought of those deadly six rifles awaiting her, and as she walked to the place of execution, she fainted. The courageous, noble-minded (!) *Herr* who was in charge, calmly drew his revolver and shot her dead where she lay. What a glorious triumph for Germany! To shoot a poor fainting hospital nurse! A woman who had given all her life to the care of others.

This incident has made a perfect furore, and a memorial fund is being started to perpetuate the memory of this noble "martyr"! Still, I think it's all being rather *over* done, and *we* shouldn't like a German woman in England getting her countrymen (who were prisoners) back to the Fatherland! But we shouldn't shoot her like a dog for all that.

OCTOBER 20TH
1915

Edith Cavell helped over 200 Allied soldiers to leave German-occupied Belgium. The story that she fainted turned out not to be true: she faced a firing-squad of eight soldiers.

·NURSE·EDITH·CAVELL·

# Thursday 21st October, 1915

Today is "our day", that is to say a day for our Red Cross Fund, and surely one could have no better object for any fund than that which looks after our wounded — who alas, are increasing at a terrible rate, as the distribution of red cross hospitals on the next page goes to prove.

One thing always strikes me as being so horrible, and that is the fact of our poor wounded men being sent out again, directly they are well enough, to the horrors of the battlefield, which they already know to their cost, while there are several great lazy louts of fellows who have done (and are doing) absolutely *nothing* for their country. But there is no doubt that before long, we shall have conscription in England. Kitchener's appeal has been nobly responded to, and our men — our true men — have given up everything to uphold our honour, for it's come to that. But still we need men — and more and *more* men.

'These little flags were sold in London all day for the good of the cause. One of them fetched 100 guineas!' the author notes.

**OCTOBER 21ST 1915**

The text of the King's letter is as follows:

Buckingham Palace.

**TO MY PEOPLE.**

At this grave moment in the struggle between my people and a highly-organised enemy, who has transgressed the laws of nations and changed the ordinance that binds civilised Europe together, I appeal to you.

I rejoice in my Empire's effort, and I feel pride in the voluntary response from my subjects all over the world who have sacrificed home, fortune and life itself in order that another may not inherit the free Empire which their ancestors and mine have built. I ask you to make good these sacrifices.

The end is not in sight. More men and yet more are wanted to keep my armies in the field, and through them to secure victory and enduring peace.

In ancient days the darkest moment has ever produced in men of our race the sternest resolve.

I ask you, men of all classes, to come forward voluntarily and take your share in the fight.

In freely responding to my appeal, you will be giving your support to our brothers who, for long months, have nobly upheld Britain's past traditions and the glory of her arms. **GEORGE, R.I.**

King George's letter to his people.

Ethel Bilbrough labels this map 'Map showing English *war hospitals* in the midland counties in Oct 1915'. The huge number of hospitals shown underlines the shocking number of casualties.

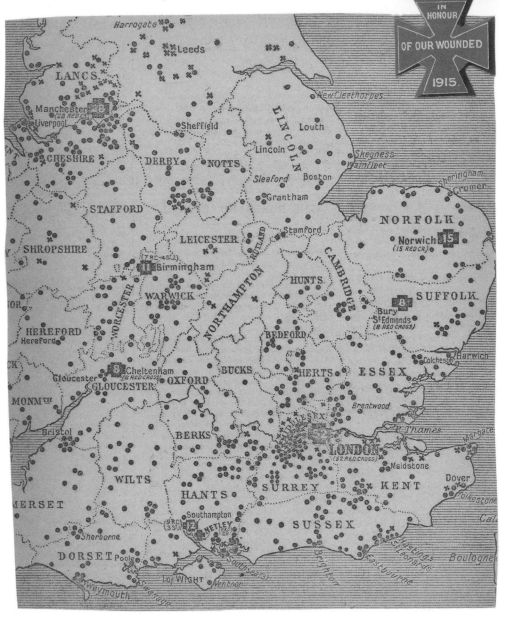

There is a rumour in the air that sooner or later we must have conscription! After all, other countries have it and I don't see why we should be exempt, and let a lot of lazy loafers hang about at home while others braver and better are doing their work. But I doubt if the present government would dare demand a big thing like conscription! Especially as it's a stupid shifting, vacillating sort of government, that can't make up its mind what to do, and it has made hideous, irretrievable blunders — such, for instance, as the Dardenelle affair, a disgrace and a cruel, wanton *waste* of brave men's lives, which are so precious today we cannot value them enough.

It is not often that one is touched *personally* by the war in comparatively small matters. But there is one way we are affected by it which is exceedingly annoying. It is when one receives a letter like this! If there is one thing more than another that a man feels a private personal *right* to, it is his own letters! But the enclosed reached one the other day, which shows how our old traditions are all being uprooted. To have strange prying curious eyes reading one's own letters (that concern no one else) is exasperating!

For some reason best known to those in authority, there has been an immense universal Registration Act passed throughout the country and every man and woman has had to give their names, ages and

## "ACCIDENTS OF WAR."

### Lord Milner Says The Blunders Must Not Be Glossed Over.

Lord Milner, in his speech at Canterbury yesterday, said that if failures and blunders like the delay to provide a sufficient supply of shells, and the barefaced attempt to conceal it, if the way in which blunder after blunder had been piled up in the Dardanelles, if the phenomenal failure of our policy in the Balkans were to be glossed over, and the nation induced to regard them as necessary accidents of the war, inevitably then we could never expect and should never deserve to see our affairs more wisely conducted in the future.

He could not understand how anybody could regard our failure to support Serbia or our belated attempt to buy the help of Greece by offering her part of our own possessions without a sense of humiliation.

Alfred Milner, 1st Viscount Milner (1854–1925), although a Tory, was one of the five members of Lloyd George's War Cabinet. Formerly High Commissioner in South Africa, he was the only Briton with experience of the civil direction of a war. He was highly critical of the incompetence of senior military officers.

The Post Office was responsible for censorship during the war, and detected many enemy agents. They caught all but one of the German spies working in the country. Fourteen spies were executed.

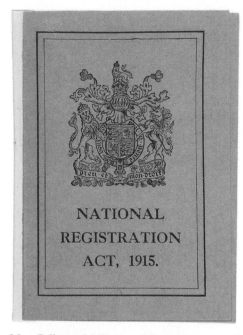

Mrs. Bilbrough's National Registration card.

occupations (old men and old women being exempt). Anyhow as it's got something to do with the war I shall stick my card in here as it's my war diary; besides I've no use for the silly thing, and why do they put "household duties" as my principal occupation in life when they certainly constitute the *least*? Just as if one was a German (ugh) frau, or a careworn "Martha"!

The other day I was rummaging among a lot of old newspapers, and found a Daily Mirror of the date of King Edward VII — giving details and pictures of his funeral. In these days, the accompanying picture is of interest. How horrified the poor dead King would have been if he could have foreseen what horrors and devilment were to emanate from the "*sorrowing* kinsman" behind his coffin!

### THE KAISER'S KISS.

**KAISER AND QUEEN-MOTHER.**

The Kaiser, still carrying his field-marshal's baton, at once ran to the other side of the carriage and with tender solicitude helped the Queen-Mother out.

Her Majesty, whose sad, pale, grief-stricken face could be seen behind her mourning veil, was a pathetic and beautiful figure. The Kaiser supported her gently and lovingly, and greeted her with a deeply affectionate kiss, which her Majesty returned.

Then the Duke of Connaught advanced, and he too kissed the Queen-Mother, who, accompanied by the Princess Victoria, the King, the Kaiser, and the Duke, then slowly passed into Westminster Hall, there to say a farewell prayer for the beloved dead.

As Queen Victoria's eldest grandchild, it was proper for the Kaiser to attend his uncle's funeral. When war came, everything the Kaiser had ever done was viewed in Britain with the deepest suspicion.

I give the picture below. Oh how little our poor grieving royal family knew then what a *Judas*, what a serpent was there, in the very midst of them all! He was a Judas even down to *the Kiss*.

No two figures attracted greater attention yesterday than King George and the German Emperor, who came to England to mark his love for his kinsman and that kinsman's realm by riding in the solemn procession, even as nine years since he

rode behind the gun-carriage on which were the mortal remains of Queen Victoria. The picture shows King George (in the centre); the Duke of Connaught, the late King's brother (nearest the camera); and the Kaiser.—(*Daily Mirror* photograph.)

'Compulsory service at last', the author notes by this cutting. Throughout the war Haselden drew a series of cartoons featuring 'Big Willie' (the Kaiser) and 'Little Willie' (the Crown Prince).

# March 5th 1916

*Conscription in England has come!* One can hardly realise it, things have come about so gradually. Voluntary recruiting did well, but not well enough, and the slackers *had* to be got at somehow, so thanks to Lord Derby's scheme, all those who wouldn't enlist will be *made* to. But the government have felt their way to this great step very cautiously, very guardedly, and have made absurd concessions relating to men bearing arms who may have *"conscientious"* objections to war! And endless exemptions are being made. On these lax lines, of course things are not working, and *far* more stringent rules must be enforced if we are to get the necessary men. Naturally every coward and slacker thinks fighting is *"wrong"* and the most ludicrous reasons are being put forward by men who want to get exemption owing to their conscientious scruples! The other day a man who said he was an artist, claimed exemption on the grounds that he *"could not mutilate anything so beautiful as the human form"*!

Only the single men have been called up so far, but compulsory service is soon to be put into practice for the young married men also.

## A Zeppelin dropping bombs.

This is really a most extraordinary photograph! It was taken during one of the *actual raids* on London! There are the search lights on it, and if you look closely, you can see the bombs in the act of falling down from the Zeppelin to the earth.

A recent photograph from Germany of one of the newest types of Zeppelins.

In December 1915 a new Q-class Zeppelin, 585 ft (178 m) long, was delivered to both the army and navy in Germany, as well as more of the existing P-class machines. Both services launched bombing raids.

**MARCH 5TH
1916**

These most vile implements of modern warfare have been rife lately, and rarely a month — or even a week passes — without a barbarous raid on some perfectly peaceful town or village, by means of which about 200 people (many of them children and babies) have been done to death, to say nothing of those who have been injured and maimed for life. What a *degrading* war this is, besides being a bloodthirsty and terrible one. The poisonous gasses, the Zeppelins, the torpedoes, and the hidden treacherous mines, all strike a note of *mean unfairness*; in modern slang it's simply "not cricket". But what does that matter to the Huns who have lost all semblance of humanity?

**WAR TIME CROP IN A CHURCHYARD.**

Potatoes instead of flowers are being grown in the churchyard of St. Catherine's, Neasdon, the vicar, curate and members of the congregation acting as sowers and reapers.

There was no rationing until very late in the war. People grew what they could to combat food shortages.

# May 1916

The most lovely month of the whole year! And never has there been a more beautiful May than this one. Yet while the birds sing and the cuckoo's note is heard continually, the sound of cannon practising intermingles with the harmony of Spring. For war still rages, and people have given up saying "when peace comes", or "when the war is ended", for at the present moment there does not appear the slightest possibility of things being settled.

Our government does nothing but wrangle and procrastinate; there has been a serious rebellion in Ireland and several people have been killed and wounded and shot, just as if we hadn't enough on hand without party politics and strife!

Never were things in such a hopeless tangle. "Compulsion *for all*" has been finally decided on, after several half-hearted attempts at it. They introduced it at first in a pitifully weak way, allowing conscientious objectors not to join the ranks! Of course, immediately hundreds of consciences awoke that had previously been dormant. But now that is all stopped, and every man will have to do something for England provided he is not past the age limit – i.e. 45 (thank goodness K. is!)

Lately a home has been opened by Arthur Pearson for those blinded in this ghastly war, and Ken has been working hard for it. He has now raised 12,000 pounds, really a colossal sum in these hard times. There was a notice in all the papers and the Daily Graphic had his picture – not half bad! Here it is – he didn't want it to go in, but I did!

During the war, Kenneth Bilbrough raised a total of £72,000 for St Dunstan's.

## A WONDERFUL COLLECTION.

### Generosity to Blinded Sailors and Soldiers

Mr. Kenneth Bilbrough, a member of Lloyd's, has during the last few weeks raised no less a sum than £11,200 for the benefit of the blinded sailors and soldiers at St. Dunstan's.

The contributors have all been connected with the commercial and insurance world, and include most of the shipping companies in the kingdom. The fact that Mr. Bilbrough was a schoolfellow of Mr. C. Arthur Pearson, at Winchester College, led him to start his collection, which prospered in a manner exceeding his most sanguine hopes. The first contributor was another Old Wykehamist.

The substantial help which has been thus secured will be principally devoted to the fund which is to be invested for the after-care of the men who have been trained at St. Dunstan's.

Mr. Kenneth Bilborough, who has raised £11,200 recently for the blinded soldiers. (Photographed by Swaine.)
(11,200)

183

# 21st May, 1916

The latest excitement has been the *Daylight Saving Bill*. Some years ago the originator of the scheme, one Willet by name who lived at Chislehurst, tried hard to get the government to adopt it, but with their usual dislike of venturing on anything new (even should it be of the utmost benefit to mankind!) they would have none of it. But now that poor Willet has been in his grave some years, and as the war has brought home to our tardy, stupid government the utmost need of saving coal and gas, the Bill was not only thought advisable, but brought in and passed. So on Saturday night, or rather on Sunday morning, the 21st May at 2 o'clock, all clocks and watches had to be set on to 3 o'clock. We altered all our time pieces however at 9.30 on Saturday evening, and then went to bed as we had made it 10.30! So we got all right without any difficulty, and without any loss of sleep! Though there were several dolts in England who "raised objections". I believe there are people who will want to argue and make objections when the Last Day comes! We benefit in many ways by the new arrangement. To begin with, in hot summer it is delightful to find at 8.30 in the morning that the air is quite bracing and fresh (it being in reality only 7.30!) and you can open every window for an hour, and so cool the house for the whole day. Then if one is shopping at 12 o'clock — usually the hottest time of the day, one is surprised to find how fresh it is, for of course it's only eleven! But the greatest benefit of all is after dinner, when it is now broad daylight till close on ten! And instead of having to get the gas lit and sit reading indoors, one can just go for a good walk, or do some gardening, or indulge in any other daylight occupation. Taking it all round, every one has reason to bless the name of Willet!

# June 2nd 1916

It has been the fashion lately for members of the feminine sex to write letters to so called lonely soldiers in the trenches! The formality of any introduction is dispensed with, and a girl may write to any Tommy or young officer she likes. A cool request from some "lonely soldiers" made my blood boil, and I answered it.

**THEIR LETTERS.**

I CANNOT help feeling that any inclination one may have felt to write to "Lonely Soldier" has been somewhat damped by his letter in *The Daily Mirror*. It is fairly obvious that the letter he likes "best of all" has nothing whatever to do with the art of penmanship. It is just the writer, the little "dream maiden," who is the attraction. Although her letter may be "crammed with cheery optimism," I venture to ask if "Lonely Soldier" would care twopence about it if he knew the sender happened to be some kindly matron or an elderly spinster anxious to do her bit.

After all, "pen letters" were asked for, but the kind of letter presumably was not specified. If a correspondence is desired merely as a means to an end in promoting the opening chapter to a "whole romantic novel," it would be more to the point if a kind of war-corresponding-matrimonial agency could be started, it being understood that no "boyish flappers," and no one over thirty need apply!
E. M. B.

Haselden's cartoon (*far right*) – which, as Ethel Bilbrough noted, came out in the Mirror the day after her letter appeared – may be a little severe. There must have been many soldiers glad to get a letter, regardless of the age of the writer!

# Saturday 3rd June, 1916

This morning comes news of our first naval battle in the great war, for up to now the Germans have kept their fleet well boxed up in port. We have lost heavily, as our main fleet was not in the North Sea where Admiral Beattie's squadron was attacked by the Enemy with her most powerful battleships, cruisers, and torpedoes, aided by three Zeppelins to throw search lights etc., and to guide them which way to go. A most unequal fight to start with, and our splendid "Queen Mary" sank in two minutes, and others followed suit before the main fleet could get up to their assistance. Our losses were appalling, about *five thousand four hundred* killed, whereas in the great battle of Trafalgar only about 400 lives were lost — far less than there were in the "Queen Mary" alone, which had over 1,000 souls. And it's dreadful to think of the poor little "middys", lads of sixteen having to go through what must have been a veritable hell upon Earth. Two Admirals killed, and 333 officers. All England is bewailing, and no wonder.

The British reverse at the Battle of Jutland was a great shock to the country. Poems like this one reflected something of the public mood.

*Opposite:* The war offered many women the chance to work for the first time. Of those who took up nursing, a large number were volunteers. Nurses were the only women who worked on the front line.

## THE YOUTHFUL DEAD.

(May 31, 1916.)
England! Stand forth and weep
For these thy dead
No more thy vigils keep,
Each noble head
Crowned with immortal praise
In flaming sea
Gives youth, love, length of days
For thee, for thee.

England! Their glory hold
Through space and Time,
Ere that brief tale be told
Arise, sublime,
And in thy Lion's might
By shore and sea
Avenge the deathless fight
With Death for thee.
—MABEL LEIGH.

# WHAT SAVED THE DELICATE DAUGHTER.

Work! Life-giving work! Instead of moping about the house, or chattering all day, thousands of well-to-do women who fancied themselves invalids have found "something to do" since the war began, and are all the healthier and happier for it.—(By Mr. W. K. Haselden.)

# June 7th, 1916

The worst news we have had since the war began reached us today, and all England is electrified with the shock — sudden and awful — that Lord Kitchener is drowned. He and his principal staff were on their way to visit Russia, and when off the Orkneys at night, and in a rough sea and gale of wind, some evil German submarine torpedoed and sank the vessel they were on, and none were saved except two of the ship's crew, who were unable to throw any light on the disaster. It has been a sad blow to England, for Kitchener was a fine man; and who but he could have raised a *voluntary* army of five million men? Everyone is feeling depressed and downhearted, for the war-lord was so trusted, and in a fierce struggle like the present war which is a struggle to the death, it is a bad thing to lose a trusted leader.

Some hours after the sad news reached England, it was all contradicted, and declared to be a mistake! And that made the disappointment all the worse when it was finally proved to be true after all.

Money raised by selling flags helped innumerable good causes associated with the war. Fund-raising flags had been sold since September 1914.

There have been so many Flag Days lately that I'm tired of entering them separately, so have devoted these pages entirely to them. It's marvellous what a lot of money is raised for the fund (whatever it may be) by the sale of these little flags which generally go for a penny each, or at most threepence. Yet some people having the cause very much at heart, have been known to give a hundred guineas for one!

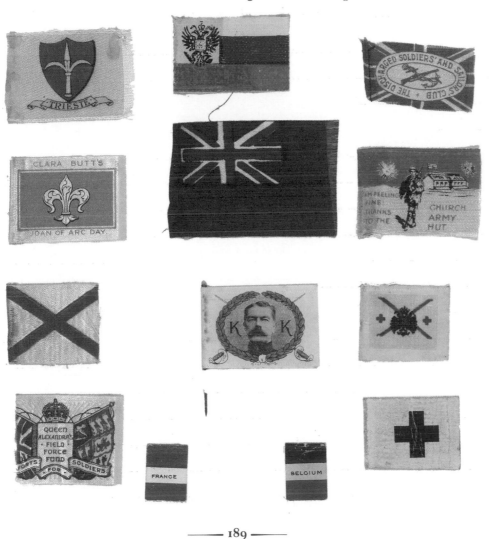

# December 14th, 1916

Another Christmas dawning! And yet no signs of peace. The butchery and the carnage, and suffering and death, continue with relentless fury. Men seem to have lost all sense of manhood and decency in their mad lust for blood.

Not only has the conflict been more deadly than ever of late, but England has been torn with political troubles at home. But a totally inefficient government couldn't be allowed to go on, and within the last few days great events have been happening. Mr Asquith has discreetly resigned and Lloyd George is now Prime Minister, and has chosen an entirely new cabinet. He is a man of *actions* (though I'd never trust a Welshman) and heaven knows the time has come when we need actions: sharp, swift, and decisive. For the last two years the government has been prevaricating, and slack, and for ever "putting off" or "waiting to see"!

Well, *we* shall see what the new Prime Minister's tactics will be! I fancy we are in for thrilling times at home!

# Friday, 19th January, 1917

So, the third year of the war has started, and as there is no sign whatever of its soon being over, I think I had better take to writing on both sides of the paper of this book, or it will mean another volume shortly!

Such an appalling disaster happened today, and as it is owing (indirectly) to this wicked awful war, I must write about it in my war diary.

Last evening I was sitting alone over the fire, just dozing comfortably after a cold and cheerless day, when without any warning there came the most ghastly crashing explosion possible to imagine! Louder than the mightiest clap of thunder. I instantly made up my mind it was a German bomb that had been intended for Woolwich, but had dropped short and fallen on our lawn instead! The house shook, windows rattled, and so deafening and alarming was it that I sat rooted to my chair, breathlessly awaiting the next shock which one felt sure would follow.

But nothing happened, and then I tore upstairs to look out of one of our upper windows which faces the direction of Woolwich, and sure enough the sky was all red and lurid and *vibrating*, and then I felt sure the arsenal was blown up and the whole of Woolwich in flames!

No news came that night, but next day we heard that it was the most awful explosion of its kind ever known, as a munition factory in East London at Silvertown had caught fire somehow (Ah! *How?*) and the fire spread till it reached all the explosives and then the whole place was hurled up into the air, and four streets were demolished, and the dead and the dying and the injured lay amongst the ruins, so that when a relief party arrived they hardly knew where to begin. A fire engine was twisted up into fragments, the unfortunate men being buried beneath.

But endless are the stories of horror — unthinkable horrors — that are gradually coming to light.

When I heard that petrifying noise I *knew* something awful was going on somewhere, and that hundreds of lives were probably being given up. And they were.

Over a hundred people were killed, and more than four hundred injured and disabled.

## 4th February, 1917

There is a saying that it is always "darkest before the dawn", and if that is true then the dawn ought *not* to be very far off! Certainly the present state of affairs could hardly be called "rosy". Germany's

Bread is now precious and every crumb is eaten. In former days it was merely broken up, not tasted, and swept away. The "crumbs that once fell from the rich man's table" now fall no more. To save in bread is the duty of rich and poor just now.—(By W. K. Haselden.)

latest act of devilry has been to issue a proclamation that she means to torpedo and sink *every single ship*, neutral or otherwise, that dares to show its face on the sea! This is to include hospital Red Cross ships, so that the poor unfortunate wounded are to be drowned like rats in a hole. Of course the whole world is in a ferment over such absolutely unparalleled brutality. But Germany is now desperate, and thinks by stopping all our imported foodstuffs, to starve us out. Of course this last move is a very serious one for England in many ways, and already there is talk in the air of the country being put on equal food rations and tickets being distributed in order to get bread and meat. The war is coming very near home . . .

# April 1917

Food is getting distinctly scarce and one begins to feel as if we were living in the days of the French Revolution! But a great deal of nonsense is written by people saying we must not think of giving even our crumbs to the poor birds. Because we are fighting against brutes must we ourselves become brutes? Feeling strongly on the matter I wrote to the Mirror this letter, though from its extremely flippant tone, I never expected to see it in print!

We have not got compulsory rations *yet*, but for the last four Sundays, in every church and chapel throughout the land, a

Ethel Bilbrough's letter points out that birds perform a valuable service. But many poor people couldn't afford bread because it was so expensive.

Large buildings were taken over by both sides for use as hospitals and rehabilitation centres. In Britain, many country houses were used in this way.

**APRIL 1917**

# HUNS USE CATHEDRAL AS A HOSPITAL.

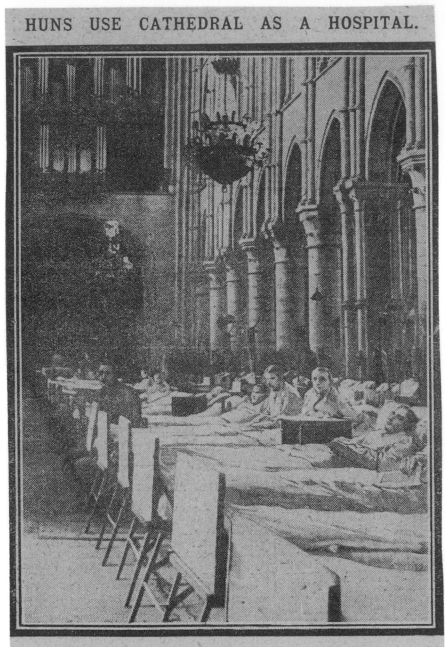

The magnificent Cathedral of Notre Dame at Laon, which dates back to the twelfth century, has been converted into a hospital for badly-wounded German soldiers. The French are now within sight of the town.

Proclamation from the King has been read exhorting the people to practise the most rigid economy, especially in bread. We are not allowed to feed our horses on corn any longer and the poor dears are growing dull and slack on hay! And dog biscuits can no longer be got for love or money, which is serious!

America has joined the fray! She couldn't well keep out of it any longer as the Germans have been calmly sinking her ships that came laden with grain to England; she certainly couldn't lay claim to her usual independence whilst that sort of thing went on. It will mean a big help to us, and a consignment of American nurses and surgeons have already arrived in England, and indeed we need them badly enough.

When I began my war diary I thought it was great extravagance buying such a large book but as I intended writing only on *one* side of the pages, I thought the war might *possibly* stretch out long enough to fill it with war incidents! But alas! The third year of war has come and there is no more sign of peace than when it just started, and I shall probably have to buy several diaries instead of one, and as paper is now ruinously dear, I must certainly write on both sides of a page in future. A friend from France writes "it seems to me we are in a dark tunnel, *sans issue*".

## Friday May 25th, 1917
### Folkestone Raid

The worst raid that we in England have experienced yet, took place in broad daylight at 5.30 today, when sixteen hostile aircraft hovered over Folkestone, dropping bombs in rapid succession. An awful scene followed. People who were doing their Whitsuntide shopping (for it's Whitsun week) were killed outright amidst the falling debris of the shops; poor old women, helpless children, babies in arms, all were ruthlessly mutilated — killed and wounded — for a bomb is no respecter of persons. 72 killed, and 114 seriously injured — oh brave, noble, *cultured* Germany!

Herbert Dale, our cousin who is vicar of Hythe — where twenty eight bombs were also dropped — was standing in the churchyard with his wife talking to the verger. The latter suddenly pointed out a fleet of aeroplanes sailing overhead — "out for practice" he said, taking them to be our men! The next minute the poor old man fell killed, and Herbert and his wife had a marvellous escape.

## FOLKESTONE AIR RAID.

### VICAR'S NARROW ESCAPE.

Many sad stories were told at the adjourned inquest yesterday on victims of the Folkestone air raid, and the jury learnt, too, of marvellous escapes. The Vicar of Hythe, the Rev. Herbert Dixon Dale, had a terrible experience. A verger, Daniel Stringer Lyth, a man of 63, was among the dead.

The vicar, giving evidence, said the verger called his attention to aircraft passing overhead. Two bombs then fell, one eighty and another forty-five yards away. Lyth was standing between witness and his wife, and fell with a cry. Immediately after, the second bomb dropped. Witness's wife was struck by a fragment near the eye. Afterwards he found a piece of metal in his own pocket, which had penetrated the cloth and was stopped by a tin box, and he providentially escaped injury. Lyth was taken to hospital, where he died.

**The Bishop Stands By.**—Here is the bomb-defying Bishop, the Bishop of Dover, who, " as an expression of sympathy with the East Coast raid sufferers, has decided to sleep at Ramsgate on moonlight nights and share the anxiety of any possible alarms." Doubtless he had an opportunity of doing a considerable amount of anxiety-sharing in the early hours of yesterday morning. This is the right spirit for the clergy, and if more of them were to show it—well, I leave it at that. —(Lafayette.)

Dr. Bilborough, the Bishop, held many important ecclesiastical appointments in the North of England, and in his youth was a great footballer.

A corner of old Folkestone.

I wrote an account of Folkestone under the heading of "The land we love" in the 'National News', as the place is very much in the public eye just at present, and here is the small drawing I did of the old town, taken from a pen and ink sketch done four or five years ago. But I heard these dear old houses are now no more.

# July 7th, 1917

A day when the war came very near home indeed. I was peacefully at work on a pen and ink drawing after breakfast — rather longing to be out in the garden among the roses, for the sun was shining and it was an ideal summer's day, when presently the whole air — the whole blue cloudless sky — seemed to become *alive*. Strange uncanny sounds came from the heights above — untranslatable sounds, but ominous and alarming in their uncertainty, and then Ada put her head round the door saying "I'm afraid there's an air raid on"; and I laid down my pen with a sinking heart and understood.

We assembled in the hall including "Jock", who immediately took the opportunity to go and have a good roll on the wet grass outside by slipping through the open door! (He knows it's forbidden!) But even if they *do* love a good roll, dogs would never dream of doing the dastardly actions the human race are at present indulging in!

Well, there was no doubt there was a raid in progress, and a pretty big one too. Overhead there was a swarm of aeroplanes looking like a flight of bees — or butterflies. But the noise! I shall never forget it. There was the peculiar steady drone of the German engines — loud enough, for they were very low down, and then came the furious banging of the machine guns showing that *our* aeroplanes had attacked the enemy and were doing their best to bring some down. Gracious heavens what next! A wild fight in the air thousands of feet above the earth! In things like fearful distorted mechanical birds (only with no beauty) which were circling round each other and engaged in deadly combat; dodging, swerving, diving and soaring, while sometimes they would be lost sight of in a cloud of smoke. There was nothing to be done; I didn't feel like going down into the cellar which people say is the safest place, but I *did* feel sick with anxiety for I knew quite well so many squadrons would *only* be sent over for one purpose — an attack on London (the last on June 13th occurred when we were away) and K's office is in the heart of the city. As we were all watching this weird and unnatural fight going on overhead there was suddenly a deafening bang quite close that made one's heart jump, and someone said "That's a bomb!" But it wasn't, it was the big cannon at Grove Park which has never been let off before. I think they fired it two or three times, and I thought every moment the house would be struck by falling shrapnel or a bomb, for it was all very close at hand. It seemed *hours* before they passed on in their mad flight and fight; in reality it must have been only about ten minutes before the sounds gradually diminished and then ceased altogether. And one looked round half dazed on a world that was still beautiful and peaceful and sunny, and wondered if it had all been a hideous nightmare? Then the thought of London returned in full force, and the next half hour of gnawing fear and anxiety I shall remember to my dying day. An awful feeling of helplessness was dominant; telephones would be off, telegraphs all stopped, how could I find out if all was well? And then a blessed boy appeared from our neighbours with a telephone message — I will give the *actual one* as a momento of a very horrible morning when the great war reached Chislehurst! Or rather the city.

**JULY 7TH**
**1917**

'Only about 200 yards from Ken's office', comments the author. Her reaction must reflect the anxieties of thousands longing for news after raids and frustrated by the lack of communications.

Air raid in
the city
Mr Kenneth
all right.

[Three bombs fell within a few yards of each other in Fenchurch-street in this first daylight raid. One five-floor block of offices was practically demolished: here 19 people were killed and five injured.

# THE WINGS OF THE TAUBE.

King Herod the n^{th}, on a distant prospect of a County Council School:—"Regardless of deir doom de liddle vigdims blay."

Drawn by EDMUND J. SULLIVAN, A.R.W.S.

Edmund Joseph Sullivan (1869-1933) was a graphic artist whose cartoons attacked German militarism. Here, the Kaiser, as a bat-winged monster rather than the 'Dove' (Taube) of the title, is represented as the Biblical child-killer Herod.

**JULY 7TH 1917**

# November 4th, 1917

Poor old England is going through dark days just now, and one cannot see the faintest prospect of peace in sight. Russia has failed us when we most needed her help, and her armies have ignominiously retreated, covered with shame instead of glory, and now the news comes that our other ally – Italy – has suffered a terrible defeat at the hands of the Huns, and two hundred thousand Italians have been taken prisoner.

In the meanwhile the inhuman barbarians who go by the name of Germans, continue to send their Gothas and their Zeppelins by stealth in the dead of night to drop their vindictive bombs on unfortunate civilians in London and the suburbs. The cowardly wickedness of such raids is almost incredible; to think of defenceless innocent women and children, and old men and boys being ruthlessly murdered and mutilated by these devils in the air is unspeakably horrible. But as someone said the other day, "There are no civilians now, we are all soldiers". Still, soldiers have the power to *hit back*, but what chance have poor frightened folk in their beds?

The odious U-boats continue to wreck and torpedo every vessel on the seas, and the number of ships and steamers that go to the bottom every week is appalling, especially when one remembers that many of them are bringing foodstuffs to England. The awful wholesale waste of it all! The fishes are having the time of their lives! And we poor Britishers have to pay the penalty in practising the most rigid economy at our tables! The extraordinary

| How household expenditure has risen since the happy days of 1914 is shown by a specimen budget which has been published, as follows:— | 1914. s. d. | 1917. s. d. |
|---|---|---|
| Bread, 4lb. loaf | 0 5 | 0 9 |
| Milk, per quart | 0 4 | 0 7 |
| Sugar, per lb. 2d to 2½ | 5½d. to 6½ |
| Butter, per lb. | 1 1 | 2 3 |
| Margarine, per lb. | 0 6 | 1 2 |
| Eggs, each | 0 1 | 0 3½ |
| Quaker oats, 2lb. packet | 0 5½ | 0 9½ |
| Tea, per lb. | 1 6 | 3 0 |
| Coal (household), per ton | 28 0 | 38 0 |
| Nestle's milk, per tin | 0 5½ | 1 0 |
| Matches, per dozen | 0 1½ | 0 11 |
| Golden syrup, 2lb. tin | 0 6½ | 1 3½ |
| Gooseberry jam, 3lb. jar | 1 4½ | 2 3 |
| Bacon (small back), per lb. | 1 2 | 2 6 |
| Mutton (Canterbury), leg or shoulder, per lb. | 0 8½ | 1 4 |
| Mutton (English), per lb. | 0 10½ | 1 6 |
| Beef (joints), per lb. 7½d. to 10½ | 1 6 |
| Wages have risen by about 30 per cent. | | |

This cutting of 2nd November 1917 shows clearly the rising cost of food. Poorer households were very hard-hit.

thing is that we aren't at the point of starvation!

Prices of course are awful, here is a little list that shows how enormously things have risen in cost since the war began. Yesterday I wanted to buy a small tinned tongue which formerly cost about 2 shillings — to my consternation the man demanded four shillings and sixpence! I walked straight out of the shop with *no* tongue beyond what nature has blessed me with gratuitously, and used it freely!

Once again Ken has been collecting for St. Dunstan's, and this year he has far surpassed his fine total of last year as will be seen by the account here given. Moreover Queen Alexandra also wrote him a personal letter of thanks, which was extremely nice of her, for it's not everyone who can claim the distinction of having received a letter of gratitude from a Queen! And written in her own hand writing, not even typed, which makes a great difference. There is something so *characterless* about a type-written letter somehow, it has come from a machine instead of a living being.

Queen Alexandra had been associated with the welfare of military men and their families ever since she had been Princess of Wales. A personal letter of thanks was much appreciated.

# ST. DUNSTAN'S HOSTEL FOR BLINDED HEROES.

## QUEEN ALEXANDRA'S LETTER TO MR. KENNETH BILBROUGH.

Her Majesty Queen Alexandra, as Patroness of St. Dunstan's Hostel for Blinded Soldiers and Sailors, has personally written a letter of thanks to Mr. Kenneth L Bilbrough, a Member of Lloyd's and an old school-fellow of Sir Arthur Pearson, expressing her very appreciative thanks for his work on behalf of the funds of St. Dunstan's.

The text of the letter, which was in her Majesty's own handwriting, is as follows :—

Sandringham,
Sept. 18, 1917.

Dear Mr. Bilbrough,

I have just heard from Sir Arthur Pearson of the truly magnificent sum of £60,000 which you have personally collected and have given to him for the present and after-care of our poor blinded soldiers and sailors, in whose behalf I am so deeply interested.

I wish to express to you my heartfelt and grateful thanks for your splendid effort on behalf of these heroes of the war, and I am proud to be the Patroness of St. Dunstan's Home, where they are so tenderly cared for and looked after by Sir Arthur Pearson, and which has now, owing to you, been so magnificently assisted in its great work.

Believe me,
Yours sincerely,
(Signed) ALEXANDRA.

The splendid sum of £67,000 has been raised in the course of two years through Mr. Bilbrough's systematic appeals to individuals and firms in the shipping, insurance, banking and commercial world, the amount in the first year aggregating £15,000.

This year Mr. Bilbrough made a further appeal for the men of St. Dunstan's, which met with a response even more liberal than the very generous one accorded to him before. A noteworthy addition to the present year's list of donors is found in the names of the two Archbishops and 34 of our Bishops, who have readily responded to and personally signed Mr. Bilbrough's appeal. Altogether Mr. Bilbrough has personally collected nearly £57,000 for the benefit of those heroes who have made so tremendous a sacrifice for the cause of their country and their Allies. Furthermore, by arousing the sympathy of influential friends he has been instrumental in securing an additional sum of about £10,000 for the funds, thereby making a total of £67,000—an achievement upon which he is to be heartily congratulated.

ST. DUNSTAN'S HOUSE
for
Soldiers & Sailors <u>blinded</u> in the War.

| | |
|---|---|
| A. F. London | 5 gns |
| Edw. Winton | 5 " |
| [?] Danesfield | 5 " |
| Edgar Alban | 3.3 |
| George Bristol | 1.1.- |
| J. A. Lichfield | 5.-.- |
| Watkin Bangor | £5-5 |
| G. W. Bath & Well: | £5.5.0 |
| Theodore Petriburg: | 1.1. |
| Handley Dunelm. | 2.2.0 |
| Herbert Newcastle | 1.1.0 |
| J. R. Roffen: | 2.2.0 |
| F. J. Liverpool | 1.1.- |
| Winifrid: O: Truron: | 1.1.0 |
| W. [?] | 1 1.0 |
| Edward S. Gloucester | 2.2.0. |
| J. Hereford | 2 0 0 |

| | |
|---|---|
| F. E. Sarum | 2.2 |
| H. R. Birmingham | 5.0 |
| [?] Ammonsbury [?] | 1.1. |
| [?] Sheffield | 1.1. |
| J. H. Ely | 5-5 |
| Hubert Southwark | 1.1 |
| Edwyn Southwell | 2 2 |
| Edward Lincoln | 1.1. |
| J. W. Carliol | 2.2 |
| C. J. Cestr | 1.1. |
| J. E. Chelmsford | 2 2 |
| E. A. Manchester | 1.0. |
| B. Norvic: | 1 1 |
| J. W. Llandaff | 1.1. |
| J. St. Davids | 1 1 |
| Hugh Worcester | 1.1. |
| H. E. Dover | 5.5 |
| Cosmo Ebor: | 5.5 |
| Randall Cantuar: | 5-5 |

# BLINDED SOLDIERS' AND SAILORS' HOSTEL.

**29887**

St. Dunstan's,
Regent's Park, N.W.

28ᵗʰ *November* 19.17

*Received* from ___ K. Bilbrough Esq. ___

*the sum of* ___ Fifty-seven thousand ___ *Pounds* ___ nine ___ *Shillings*
*and seventy four*

*and* ___ *Pence.*

Arthur Pearson

£57074 : 9 : —

'Original receipt for fifty-seven thousand pounds
(*collected by K. L. Bilbrough*) & signed by Sir Arthur
Pearson (first instalment only)' – definitely a
receipt to be saved for Ethel Bilbrough's War Diary!

*Left:* Ethel Bilbrough notes 'original signatures of 34
English bishops, concluding with the Archbishops
of York and Canterbury' — a tribute to her husband's
persuasive fund-raising powers.

# November 1917

Two bad reverses have befallen the Allies this month, the worst being the total collapse of Russia, which, consumed by revolution and anarchy, has broken its treaty and turned traitor to the Allies, offering a separate peace to Germany. This is a blow, as it will liberate all the German soldiers kept in Russia now, who will return to reinforce their regiments at the front. One has no words for Russia, her mean cowardly conduct is unspeakable.

Then Italy. For a long while no one heard much about Italy, and then quite suddenly the Italians started *retreating*, in other words running away! Or throwing up their hands as a sign of capitulation. And so we and the French have had to send whole armies to help them when all the time we need every single man we have to help in France.

Oh this war! Will the end of it ever come? Peace seems farther off than ever, and our men freeze in the bitter cold of the trenches and the flower of our land is getting ruthlessly slain and slaughtered day by day — oh the *pity* of it all, the wicked waste of fresh young lives, and the misery and wreckage their deaths leave in thousands of broken hearts, to whom nothing will ever be the same again. It is terrible to see how lengthy the list grows in the little war shrine at church (even in a small place like this) for those who have laid down their lives for King and country.

And it is hard for those left who still struggle bravely on, to put Patriotism before Peace. But a peace now would *not* be an honourable one or a lasting one, because were a treaty even possible, we know by past experience that Germany has no respect for either treaties or honour.

But how in Heaven's name will it all end? And *when*?

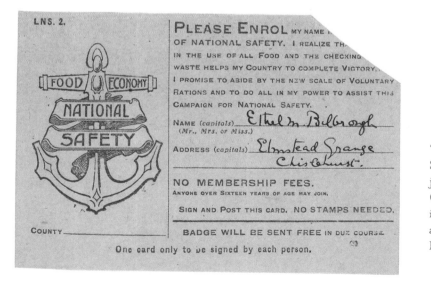

'From Sir Arthur Yapp (to me!)' the
author notes. Sir Arthur Keysall
Yapp (1869-1936) was National
Secretary of the YMCA, which was
helping sailors and men on the
front line.

'"League of National
Safety" of which I have
just become a member!
(The object of the league
is *voluntary* economy
and rationing)' Ethel
Bilbrough explains.

# January 1918

The Christmas of 1917 has come and gone, and we have now entered upon our fourth year of war. One feels thankful that the old year has departed, and no one will ever look back on 1917 without a thrill of horror.

The King and Queen have sent such nice messages at this time to the Empire's fighters, that I give it word for word.

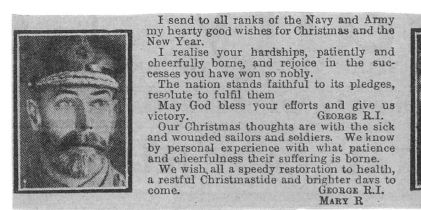

I send to all ranks of the Navy and Army my hearty good wishes for Christmas and the New Year.

I realise your hardships, patiently and cheerfully borne, and rejoice in the successes you have won so nobly.

The nation stands faithful to its pledges, resolute to fulfil them

May God bless your efforts and give us victory. GEORGE R.I.

Our Christmas thoughts are with the sick and wounded sailors and soldiers. We know by personal experience with what patience and cheerfulness their suffering is borne.

We wish all a speedy restoration to health, a restful Christmastide and brighter days to come. GEORGE R.I.
MARY R

George V had visited the men on the Western Front, and seen the conditions they endured. Royal Christmas messages were designed to keep up the morale of the troops.

Poor King George! He must often feel he would gladly change places with any irresponsible crossing sweeper in the land! No English King has ever found himself in such an awful world-wide struggle before.

One wonders what the New Year 1918 will bring? It is bound to be a year of crisis, for food supplies are running short and the enemy that we shall all have to fight before very long will be famine and starvation if the present state of things continues. And yet every day more and more ships are sunk by the dastardly U-boats, and millions of tons of priceless foodstuffs go to the bottom of the sea.

Meat is getting scarce and we have had no butter or margarine for a fortnight! I am rather glad, because when one is struggling with a slice of horrid dry toast that rebels against going down, one really feels one is at last taking part in the war! How *poor* people live is a mystery! For fish is ruinous, and in a little Kentish village rabbits were being sold for 6 shillings and 10 shillings apiece! And now this week one reads in the paper of a fowl going for 15 shillings! Worst of all, the Englishman's standby – bacon – is unprocurable!

But all this is vastly insignificant in comparison to air raids, which everyone lives in terror of when the moon gets full! I hate to see that bright white light at night, for with it one expects every moment to hear the horrible sound of engines overhead, and the booming of great guns close at hand – ugh!

# January 19th, 1918

This morning I was somewhat nonplussed by Ada bringing me the information that the butcher had come but had *no* meat for our lunch! As it was then past twelve, things didn't look  promising, moreover being a Saturday the "cupboard was bare" – as it usually is at the end of the week. I had to dress hurriedly, catch up a basket, and depart for the village in order to forage for a meal. Mercifully fowls still produce eggs though butchers have ceased to produce meat, and *they* (the fowls) didn't fail me. But it looks ominous for the future, and things are getting harder and harder – especially for the poor, and I think it's *exasperating* of Lord Rhonda to calmly accuse the people of being "greedy growsers" (his own words) when there's no meat, and precious little fish (and at a prohibitive price), and no cheese, nor bacon, nor butter, nor margarine, nor marmalade, nor jam, nor sugar! "Greedy growsers" indeed! Like that silly statesman (I forget his name) who, after some horrible air raid in which several people were killed and mutilated and injured, accused the multitude of being a set of *"squealing jays"*! I never hear a harsh voiced jay now (and we have several about our garden), without thinking of the imbecility of government officials!

# January 23rd, 1918

If it weren't for all the horrors of this awful war, the present situation here at home might certainly be said to have its humorous side! The idea of our stolid British householders having to forego their everlasting Sunday joint (which hitherto has been regarded as unalterable as the law of gravity!) and to do without butter, and to sit down to a baconless breakfast, *is* all really very comic. There's one thing an Englishman (or woman) does not shine at, and that is in adapting themselves to changed circumstances. We are all hugely conservative, and imagine that the things which have become *habitual* are equally unchangeable.

The butchers shops have all been closed now for four days, and it's said there is no prospect of their opening again for a considerable time, which is not to be wondered at as they can get no meat at the markets!

Yesterday we hadn't a morsel of bread in the house, and I had to order the carriage and go and fetch, and bring home the loaves myself! Lean people will turn into skeletons at this rate, and fat people will get quite good figures!

# Monday 28th January, 1918

*It is twelve o'clock at night!* A strange hour to be writing in a diary, but we are sitting up – Ken and I – after a most horrible air raid, waiting for the "all clear" signal to go (which it *won't* do), and yet there have been no guns for over an hour. And we are waiting too for Puncher's return – who is a special constable – and who always gets back soon after all is quiet. The firing began tonight just as we were finishing dinner, the sickening "ping-g-g" that one knows so well sounded just as I was starting on an apple (that never got eaten)! And then it all went on intermittently for about two hours and a half, and at 9.30 the noise was *awful!* The barrage sounded as if it was on our lawn, and we saw the shells breaking up in the sky just like shattered stars (unpleasantly near).

We are getting dreadfully sleepy with the horrid *wakeful* sleepiness that follows some great mental excitement. Ten minutes past twelve! Why *doesn't* Puncher come? Ken puts on more coals, and I tried to knit, but dropped so many stitches I soon threw it aside.

(*Next day*) I had to give up writing here as it was getting decidedly cold, and we drew up our chairs to the fire and watched the clock. Twelve thirty came — we were utterly mystified — and then through the silence rang out a quick *bang-bang* horribly loud and like a sort of bark! One's heart sank! They were *coming back*! It was all about to recommence, when we were dead with sleep, and chilled all through. The "barking" continued, and the great window on the stairs shook all over, and so did the front door (and so did I)! We understood at last why the "all clear" bugle had not been sounded, and why Puncher had not returned.

Firing continued, and at 1.15 Ada came in with some hot tea, and then at 1.30 we heard — oh! so thankfully — the "all clear" signal sound and, tired and raid-racked we toiled up to bed, where I lay till morning *wide* awake, and thinking of all the horrors those fiendish Gothas had accomplished in their hellish night's work.

The papers said 58 were killed and about 200 injured, but they keep things back, and all the raid news is now suppressed. But many terrible things happened in London, amongst others a panic took place in one of the tube shelters and fourteen people (including seven children) were trampled to death. A bomb struck a high building where there were huge water tanks which crashed straight down into the cellars, where thirty people had taken refuge. They were all killed, and most of them were drowned.

Apart from any personal fear during these hateful raids, one cannot help feeling *sick* with apprehension as to what is going on (assuredly) *somewhere*, all the while one listens to the incessant booming of the guns, sometimes near at hand, sometimes far off. And for nights afterwards the sound seems to recur, and it eats into one's brain in the still hours of the night, however much one may fight against it. A powerful imagination is a tiresome thing to have! But it's temperamental (if there's such a word!) and sometimes it helps one to picture *nice* things very vividly, so on the whole it has its compensations, like everything else.

# March, 1918

The fierce "starlight raid" which took place on the night of Thursday 7th March, brought the horrors of it very near home, for a bomb was dropped almost within a stone's throw of my brother's house in Randolph Crescent. No one was in the least expecting a raid as there was no moon, only bright starlight, and everyone was more or less astounded when the maroon went off soon after eleven. As an "eye witness" account of a thing is always more interesting (and more reliable) than an outsider's, I will quote word for word from my brother's letter the day after the raid. He writes this; "Thank God we are all alive! But it has been a near thing. We got the "warning" at 11.20, and went down into the basement; the guns had only just started when there was the most appallingly awful crash that is possible to describe. Lilian was hit on the head by a bit of plaster but mercifully it was nothing serious, and they were all very brave. The houses struck (just the other side of the gardens) are *gone*, and every home in the crescent is wrecked. After the "all clear" had gone I recollect forcing back the billiard room door (smashed off its hinges, and piled with debris) and then we saw that awful sight of the houses across the garden *all on fire*, and reduced to ruins, many poor imprisoned people being below and powerless to get out, and I shall never forget their heart-rending screams to my dying day. All night long, hundreds of rescuers were working furiously, but it was over 15 hours before many bodies could be recovered. Our vicar worked magnificently and so did a local doctor who managed to pump oxygen down a pipe to those who were being suffocated by the heaps of debris beneath which they were buried" . . . !

This from the pen of one's *own brother* makes one *realise* things far more than reading it from some newspaper's account, which are rarely reliable. Of course the raid left their home uninhabitable, and they have migrated to a peaceful riverside residence in the Thames Valley! And I don't think, after such a ghastly experience, they will ever care to spend another night in London while the war lasts. (N.B. To come very near death, teaches one to value life).

## Good Friday – 29th March, 1918

The last ghastly and inhuman act the Germans have perpetrated has been the shelling of a church in Paris (on Good Friday), which was filled with people taking part in the most sacred and the most solemn service of the year.

The Huns have just introduced a new abomination in the shape of a long range gun – or "mystery gun" as it goes by the name of here – which can fire its shells 80 or 90 miles. And they are bombarding Paris daily, and if they got to Calais, they would turn it on to London.

*Right:* 'National News: Easter Sunday'. Ethel Bilbrough's clipping describes the Paris Gun, the biggest gun used during the war. It took 80 men to fire a shell weighing 210 lb (94 kg) that could travel 81 miles (130 km).

Dr. Fritz Rauserberger, who, it is stated, is the designer of the long-range gun which has been shelling Paris

*Left:* Prof. Dr Fritz Rausenberger (1868-1926) was Director of Design for the German gun manufacturer Krupps. As well as the Paris Gun, he also designed 'Big Bertha'. Mrs Bilbrough writes: 'Note his horrible "long-range" head!'

# LONG-RANGE GUN TRAGEDY.

## PARIS CHURCH STRUCK BY SHELL. *during Good Friday*

### 75 WORSHIPPERS KILLED.

PARIS, Saturday.

A shell fired by the German long-range gun struck a church in the Paris district during a Good Friday service. Seventy-five of the congregation were killed and ninety were wounded, including a great number of women and children. Among those killed were M. Stroehling, Councillor of the Swiss Legation, and Madame Stroehling, Brigadier-General Francfort, of the Reserves, Dr. Delouvrier, Dr. Mendelssohn, Count Jean Maussion and Miss Comingham.

It was about 4 p.m. that a violent detonation was heard. The shell smashed through the vaulted roof, making a breach of from five to six square yards. A mass of stones and brickwork was sent flying into the nave, crushing a great number of persons.

### SCENES OF DESTRUCTION.

The frightful noise caused by the bursting of the shell shook the church to its foundations, causing a large portion of the arches and the left side of the nave to collapse. Cries of horror from the terror-stricken worshippers filled the church. The shell struck one of the large pillars between the windows which sustain the roof, causing it to collapse, and bringing the arch down. Stones and heavy material came down from a height of sixty feet, falling on the congregation. Splinters and portions of the exploded shell flew about in all directions. Some fragments of the metal struck the walls of the nave and the organ and ricocheted to the choir stalls.

By 5 p.m. close on sixty wounded victims had been taken to hospital and forty corpses removed from the ruins. These figures grew as helpers continued to search amongst the debris, and finally numbered seventy-five dead and ninety injured. When President Poincaré arrived there were already present the Prefect of Police and Cardinal Amette, the Archbishop of Paris, who stood gazing with eyes filled with tears at the terrible spectacle which confronted them.

"The wretches—the wretches," cried the Archbishop, "they have chosen the day and the hour Christ died on the Cross to commit this crime."

The Abbé of the church stated in an interview that a sacred concert was about to be given in the church, where the choristers were already assembled. When the first notes of the organ pealed out the church was crowded. Suddenly the brutal crime was perpetrated. "It is horrible," commented the Abbé, "and I still ask myself if I am not suffering from some ghastly nightmare."—Exchange.

# Easter — 30th March, 1918

The "great push" by the Germans on the Western Front which everyone has been feverishly waiting for, has commenced at last, and the Huns in appalling numbers are hurling themselves on our lines, mad to break through. Never has there been a more anxious or critical time in the whole war, and we daily hold our breath for news. Our poor brave boys are far outweighed in numbers by the Germans, who have endless fresh divisions always coming up, and it is three to one. Already they have forced us back, but the Allies are making a fine stand in spite of the heavy odds against them.

MARCH 30TH
1918

The Germans thought the Paris Gun would have a bad psychological effect on the French.

## THE RUINED CRECHE—KULTUR'S LATEST TRIUMPH!

Last Friday, during the bombardment of Paris by the long-range gun, one of the shells struck a crèche, with the result that four persons were killed and twenty-one wounded. The wrecked dormitory, showing where the shell entered.

# June 1918

Lord Rhonda, the great Food Controller, has just died. Poor man! He had rationed himself too severely, and when he got ill with pleurisy or something, he had no strength left to fight against it. But he will be much missed for he worked out the appalling problem of placing England under food rations with amazing skill and foresight. It was he who introduced the ration cards which every soul has had; no one could get any meat or butter or bacon or poultry without presenting in exchange an absurd little paper coupon. Neither at a restaurant nor an hotel may one procure meat without one, though "a half portion" is permitted, in which case the coupon is divided! In years to come people will hardly believe that such things really *were*, and yet they not only exist at the present day, but the whole scheme has succeeded wonderfully well, in spite of the stupendous difficulties that had to be overcome.

*Here is a genuine meat "coupon" of the Great War* (some people always call them "Kupongs")! – it would buy meat to the value of *five pence only*, and each person is allowed three meat coupons per week, so we don't get fat on *that*!

Rationing was finally introduced in February 1918. This coupon, representing fivepence-worth of meat, would be worth 2½ pence today, though the value of money has changed enormously.

Why in the world should we adopt the French word "coupon" I wonder? And the funny thing is that the French have adopted an *English* one for the same thing, and talk about their "tickets"!

Things look about as gloomy as they possibly can. The sinking of our ships (*daily*) by the German submarines, continues in appalling numbers. The pent-up fury of the Huns is all being concentrated in their last "Great Offensive", and our lines are broken badly at the front, yet our brave boys remain undaunted, and continue the struggle valiantly against tremendous odds. I keep thinking of Watts' picture of "Hope"; it is strangely applicable to the present time. We may be downcast (and certainly *are*) but there is always that deathless stirring of "Hope" left, though all else seems shattered and tottering! Fortunately the thought of *England conquered* is *un*thinkable (which sounds rather a paradox)!

The Kaiser has (with his usual *humility*) announced his intention of completely "crushing" the British Army!

*Mrs Bilbrough writes:* Hole on Paul's Cray Common (and now filled up with water), which was caused by a bomb from enemy aircraft overhead, on the night of May 19th, 1918, during a raid.

# Spring 1918 (June)

The weather is nearly as depressing as the war news; the rain and the cold chill one, as does the fact that the Germans are gradually but steadily pushing nearer to Paris day by day. This unfortunate city is much worse off than London, for it is relentlessly shelled by "Big Bertha" (the long range gun) during the day, and bombed by relays of Gothas during the night!

The last London raid occurred on May 19th, but thank goodness we were many miles away, safe in peaceful Glastonbury! It began at eleven at night and was one of the worst raids we have experienced; nearly fifty people were killed and over 161 injured.

Chislehurst too came in for some bombing on this occasion; one bomb was dropped on Paul's Cray Common, and another just outside the Parish Church, which mercifully fell in the grass of the Common, and did no damage beyond breaking the windows all round, and making a large hole in the Common, not *quite* as big as its rival excavation, the cockpit! Which is only a few feet away!

It makes the war seem horribly real when these nerve-shattering bombs are dropped at one's very door! (See opposite.)

# June 4th

The postage rate has now been increased as a means of extra taxation, and from today no more letters will be sent for a penny. They will all be three halfpence, and postcards will be one penny instead of a halfpenny. Shan't write so many letters in future!

# June 14th

This morning we were all busy at the hospital depot helping to make such queer garments. They are intended for our *snipers* at the Front, and are like great shapeless bags of coarse linen canvas. When they are stitched together they go to London, where they are painted by various artists all sorts of colours representing earth, twigs, and grass, in order to mystify and deceive the enemy. The snipers also wear helmets with tufts of grass and moss stuck into them, and, when they are completely turned out, what horrid uncanny looking objects they must be! Creeping stealthily along the enemies' lines under cover of the darkness.

Thank goodness America has at length intervened and is now drawn into this vast worldwide struggle, and *not a moment too soon*, for even the cheeriest optimists have been going about with long faces lately, and we have hardly dared to look ahead. But now this great country has come to the aid of the Allies — and also to preserve her own shipping, which the Germans have been ruthlessly destroying by their U-boats, when it came in their way — but now WE SHALL SEE!

# Sunday, 4th August, 1918

A lovely day which was fortunate, as being the fourth anniversary of the war, a special form of service has been drawn up to be held throughout the land, and ours took place in the old cockpit on the Common! Truly the war has worked wonders and conventionalities are no longer regarded as they were. The service was held by the Rector, the Vicar, and the Wesleyan minister! Who wisely forgot their doctrinal differences, and agreed to meet as fellow Christians and brothers, thinking of nothing but the widespread need for prayer just now for everyone, apart from any sect or creed. The cockpit was filled to overflowing with a very quiet and well behaved congregation who extended over a greater part of the Common as well. The three clerics were all in plain white surplices (which looked queer blowing about in the wind), the rector and vicar had abandoned stoles and cassocks and birettas and other ritual garments, while the Wesleyan minister had consented to put on a white surplice for the first time in his life! It was a very impressive service, held under the blue sky of heaven, and once an aeroplane flew low, right over our very heads, and I couldn't help thinking, "suppose it's an enemy one, come to drop bombs on this vast concourse of people"! But nothing happened, and even the rain kept off, which would have been nothing short of a calamity as no one had brought umbrellas, in spite of some rather ominous thunder clouds hanging about.

The rector opened the service by reading the following, and all the people kept so quiet you could have heard a pin drop.

"Brethren, on this fourth anniversary of the declaration of War, let us draw near to God in penitence and humility; let us pray Him to deliver us from the temptations that beset us and, if it be His Will, to grant us victory and peace. Let us implore His help for all those who are engaged at home or abroad in carrying on the war, and let us thank Him for mercies already vouchsafed to us." Then followed a special litany and prayers, and a few well known hymns like "Oh God Our Help in Ages Past" and "Holy Father in Thy Keeping" and others, and then we all walked home to tea in a suitable and orderly manner! It's a pity we don't have more out of door services, the people like them and behave well, but of course there's always the danger of a few black sheep being about and causing disturbances, and the uncertainty of our English climate is a drawback which cannot be overcome.

# July 16th, 1918*

The Germans have begun their *third* great offensive, and thank heaven the Allies are holding their own, and in some cases we have even driven the enemy back. The poor dethroned Tzar of Russia has just been shot, and all Russia is in a state of frenzied revolution and disorder.

# August

Things begin to look ever so much brighter than they did, and everyone is going about with a much lighter step and a much lighter heart. Several towns which we lost in the last offensive, such as Soissons, Bapaume, and Péronne, have all been regained. In one's own imagination one is inclined to think of these places as still intact, but an interesting letter from a friend in France, Col. H. Fortescue, throws light on the subject. He writes — "The desolation of Northern France is simply indescribable. An absolutely dead world, with no signs of life anywhere. Miles upon miles of dead trees, not a village to be seen, for they are all gone. There is literally not a trace of all those villages and towns, the names of which you read of daily in the papers as being "retaken". Bapaume, Péronne, etc., are a mere heap of stones. Arras is a complete ruin, not a single house left habitable. Amiens has suffered a good deal of damage, particularly in the principal street and round the Cathedral, which by some extraordinary coincidence has practically remained uninjured. The only damage I could see to it was where one field gun shell had fallen through the roof, to become embedded in the pavement of the nave beneath . . ."

* Ethel Bilbrough backdates this diary entry to July, in order to comment on the German third offensive.

# October 1918

This has been a most eventful month, and it seems impossible to believe that the end is in sight at last. Is it really true that after these four interminable years of uphill fighting and grappling against tremendous odds, that we are finally *going to win*? No Englishman would ever admit it, not even to himself, but I believe there have been times in the war when the paralysing thought has flashed through our minds that we were going to get — well, that we were *not* going to win!

But now all is changed. America's timely help came just when it was most needed, and it also inspired the Allies to buck up and fight with redoubled zeal and deathless courage.

At the beginning of the month Bulgaria caved in, and on the 28th, Austria (who has been getting dreadfully tired of fighting for a long while past) pleaded desperately for a separate peace. Turkey was the next enemy to throw up the sponge, and on the 31st of this month an armistice was signed between us.

So, taking it all round, it's been a wonderful month, and now the whole world is watching with breathless interest the moves of President Wilson and the great Field Marshal, Foch — who is a fine French man. After all, military manoeuvres very much resemble a complicated game of chess — only the pawns are living souls unhappily.

*Right, top:* Woodrow Wilson (1856-1924) 28th President of the USA, did not wish to join the war, but German attacks on American shipping brought the United States in with the Allies in 1917. The Americans pursued the war vigorously, making a critical difference to the result.
*Right:* Ferdinand Foch (1851-1929) was thought by many to be the greatest Allied general of the war. By April 1918, Foch was in command of the Allied armies. He stopped a strong German attack into France, and counterattacked, driving the Germans back into Belgium.

Mr. Wilson, who is expected to land in France on Thursday and will afterwards visit England. He is the first American President to visit Europe whilst in office. —*Stanley.*

Marshal Foch, who, as supreme commander of the Allies forces, announces armistice terms to German envoys.

We must salute also the great general, Marshal Foch, to whom, more than to any living man, we owe it that to-day—instead of to-morrow, instead of months and years hence—the nightmare is lifted from our minds.

# KAISER ABDICATES :

The above startling words appeared in this morning's Sunday paper, and needless to say, they have thrown us all into a state of thrilling expectancy and pent-up excitement. A report was also circulated that the Armistice between Germany and the Allies had been signed — which would of course mean the end of hostilities and — peace! But there was nothing authentic to go by, and the day passed with no further reliable news, though the Kaiser's abdication (which is official) is good enough news for one day! And that little worm — the crown prince — has also made a bolt of it. They even desert their precious "Fatherland" directly it is in sore straits.

I expect tomorrow we shall get the finest, most splendid news of all, that the Armistice is really and truly signed.

**NOVEMBER 10TH 1918**

*The Kaiser!*

Wilhelm II of Germany (1859-1941) was bellicose and impetuous. He was not a particularly good war leader. When he lost the support of the German Army, he abdicated, going into exile at Doorn in the Netherlands.

*King George*
## "GOD SAVE THE KING."

George V (1865-1935) was the second son of Edward VII. He was heavily influenced by his service in the Navy as a young man. Anti-German feeling was so great during the First World War that he renounced all his German titles and decorations and announced that his family would be called Windsor — a popular move.

### NOVEMBER 10TH
### 1918

The "All-Highest", the "War Lord"! *Dethroned, crushed, conquered, humiliated, disgraced;* and loathed now and for evermore for the countless crimes he has committed, the unspeakable cruelties he has condoned and the millions of human beings he has slain throughout Europe.

# Monday, 11th November 1918  PEACE!

The armistice is signed, *"the day"* has come at last! And — it is *ours*! Every heart is vibrating to the wonderful song of Triumph that swells throughout the Empire this day. *The war is over!* And *we have won the war*, and glory, honour and victory is ours.

**War's Last Chantey.**

"Thanks be to GOD Who giveth us the
Victory!"
So they sang of old, and the song is ours
to-day:
Ended our toil, our unutterable weariness,
Lifted our load, our peril passed away!

## Monday 11th November (*continued*)

More than four years ago at the outset of the war, when all England
was thrilling with excitement, I bought this small Union Jack,
and stuck it up over the mantelpiece. There it stayed some weeks,
getting dusty — but still preserving a patriotic look! Then came a
day (soon after the retreat from Mons), when all flags and such-
like festive emblems, fell flat somehow. Anxiety had replaced
patriotism in a sense, and I surreptitiously removed my small flag,

with a mental vow that it should only reappear when old England had won through! And *now that time has come!* Yet how little I dreamed then that it would be four long weary years of drawn out suspense and agony (when even defeat would sometimes stare us in the face) before right could conquer might. So I have put this small trophy in my war diary, because it is really quite a historic little flag, and could tell a tale of the great war to succeeding generations from beginning to end, almost from that crucial moment when the edict went forth, "England has sent an ultimatum to Germany", down to the signing of the armistice this morning!

Today has been a truly wonderful day, and I'm glad I was alive to see it! From the moment one got out of bed, this 11th of November, there was a sort of feeling *in the air* that *something* was going to happen! And yet we all felt doubtful of Germany up to the very last, and half expected some new act of treachery at the eleventh hour. I was trying to write a coherent letter this morning (rather a difficult proceeding under the circumstances!) when all of a sudden the air was rent by a tremendous *BANG!* My instant thought was — *a raid!* For our maroons have become so interwoven with the horrors of Gothas and bombs that it has become almost impossible to disassociate them. But when another great explosion shook the windows, and the hooters at Woolwich began to scream like things demented, and the guns started frantically firing all round us like an almighty fugue, I knew that this was no raid, but that the signing of the armistice had been *accomplished!* Signal upon signal took up the news, the glorious pulverising news, that the end had come at last, and *the greatest war in history was over.*

London went quite mad and let itself go. Pandemonium reigned everywhere; bells burst out into chimes, guns "volleyed and thundered", sirens and hooters screamed, while people sang, waved, cheered, shouted, rang dinner bells, and lost their heads generally!

But I think the most impressive sight of all must have been

that in front of Buckingham Palace. Here vast crowds assembled, all shouting out at the tops of their voices *We want the King*"! So the King and Queen, and young Princess Mary, came out on to the balcony to be greeted by a roar of cheers, and when the King could be heard he said;

"With you I rejoice and thank God for the victories which the allied armies have won, bringing hostilities to an end, and peace within sight". And even our usually self-contained Queen grew excited and waved a flag! And they must all have felt pretty chokey, what with their thousands of loyal subjects all round them waving and yelling, and the bands playing "God save the King" and the "Old Hundredth"! Even to read about it all in the papers makes one feel like crying! This historic scene terminated by the band striking up "Old Lang Syne", and then King George, waving his hat, went back into the Palace followed by the Queen and "little Mary"!

*And I guess they all said their prayers that night.*

**NOVEMBER 11TH
1918**

Many people must have wondered how they had endured those years, weeks and days.

PEACE.

Bow down, Old Land, at the altar-steps of
    God —
Thank Him for Peace, thank Him for
    Victory;
But thank Him chiefly that thy feet have
    trod
The path of honour, in the Agony.

                              J. S. ARKWRIGHT.

Sir John Stanhope Arkwright
(1872-1954) politician, poet and
horticulturalist, is best known for writing
the hymn 'O valiant hearts'.

## NOVEMBER 11TH
## 1918

A useful aid to memory — but this short diary doesn't give any clue about lives
lost or devastation caused.

# DIARY OF THE GREAT WAR.

**1914.**

July   28—Austria-Hungary declares war on Serbia.
Aug.    1—Germany declares war on Russia.
 ,,     3—Germany declares war on France.
 ,,     4—Great Britain declares war on Germany.
 ,,    12—State of war declared between Great
            Britain and Austria-Hungary.
 ,,    16—Expeditionary force landed in France.
 ,,    23—Japan declares war on Germany.
Sept.   5—End of retreat from Mons to Marne.
Nov.    5—Great Britain declares war on Turkey.
Dec.    8—Naval battle off Falkland.

**1915.**

April  27—Allied troops land in Gallipoli.
May     7—Lusitania torpedoed.
 ,,    13—Italy declares war on Austria.
 ,,    25—Coalition Cabinet formed.
July    9—Conquest of German South-West Africa.
Oct.   13—Nurse Cavell murdered by Germans.
 ,,    14—Bulgaria at war with Serbia.

**1916.**

Jan.    8—Complete evacuation of Gallipoli.
May     3—Compulsory Military Service Bill.
 ,,    31—Battle of Jutland.
June    5—Lord Kitchener drowned.
July    1—Somme battle began.
 ,,    27—Captain Fryatt shot by Germans.
Aug.   27—Rumania declares war on Austria-Hun-
            gary. Italy declares war on Germany.
Dec.    7—Mr. Lloyd George Prime Minister.

**1917.**

March  11—British take Bagdad.
 ,,    12—Revolution in Russia.
April   5—United States at war with Germany.
Nov.   18—General Maude, victor of Bagdad, died in
            Mesopotamia.
Dec.    9—Fall of Jerusalem.

**1918.**

March   3—Treaty of Brest-Litovsk concluded be-
            tween Germans and Bolsheviks.
 ,,    21—Kaiser's battle to " crush " British Army
            opens on fifty-mile front.
April   9—Mr. Lloyd George introduced Bill rais-
            ing Army age to fifty.—(Passed.)
July   16—Tsar shot by Bolsheviks.
 ,,    18—Great French counter-attack begins.
Aug.    8—Sir D. Haig attacks on twenty-mile front.
Sept.  15—Austria's offer to discuss peace.
 ,,    30—Bulgaria surrenders unconditionally.
Oct.    6—Germany, Austria and Turkey seek peace
            through President Wilson.
 ,,    17—British naval force landed at Ostend.
            Lille captured by British.
 ,,    27—Ludendorff resigns.
 ,,    28—Austria pleads for separate peace.
 ,,    31—Allied armistice with Turkey.
Nov.    4—Armistice with Austria takes effect.
 ,,     9—Kaiser abdicates. Crown Prince also
            signs a renunciation.
 ,,    11—Armistice signed at 5 a.m. Hostilities
            cease at 11 a.m.

'Big' and 'Little' Willie kicked out — with ordinary shoes, not military boots. The small windmills on the left indicate their destination in the Netherlands.

NOVEMBER 11TH 1918

THE END OF THE WILLIES.

Christmas good wishes in 1918 must have been more than usually heartfelt.

We'll meet the Future
full of Faith and Hope.

1914-1915.

Christmas Greetings
& all Good Wishes
for the coming
Year

from

THE EDITOR & STAFF
OF
"THE AFRICAN WORLD,"
LONDON, E.C.

PRODUCED IN ENGLAND.

# Index

Page references in *italics* refer to the transcript version